W9-COJ-633

52 Weeks Of

Gratitude

Journal

Kim Richardson
Publishing

52 Weeks of Gratitude Journal

Kim Richardson
Publishing

Contact: kim.richardson@kimrichardson.kim

Compiled by: Kim Richardson
Foreword by: Sunny Dawn Johnston
Cover Design: Kim Richardson
Cover Photo Credit: Creative common image at Pixabay.com
Illustrations and Coloring Pages: Creative common images at Pixabay.com unless otherwise stated

CONTENTS

FOREWORD

Welcome my friend! By choosing to read this book you have gifted yourself with an opportunity to truly change your life. If you have practiced gratitude on and off, then you know how good it feels. And, if you've practiced gratitude consistently, well, then you know what a truly powerful force it is. I have been a gratitude appreciator most of my adult life and I know how much the simple act of embracing and embodying gratitude has changed me.

I am grateful that you are reading this book right now. Why? Because I believe that gratitude can change the world. I believe I speak for all of the authors, including my friend and the visionary behind this book, Kim Richardson, when I say that the more of us who are filled with gratitude, are intentional, are focused on having an open and grateful heart, the more potential there is for our world to experience Peace ON Earth. So, THANK YOU for picking up this book and contributing to the healing of our world, one beautiful heart at a time.

Gratitude, by definition, is the state of being grateful; it's that warm and friendly feeling toward a benefactor; the kindness awakened by a favor received; and even thankfulness for a life challenge. I've often said - and have heard many times as well - that "Thank you" is the greatest prayer ever spoken. Therefore, to me, gratitude IS prayer.

Kim has taken three of the greatest healing elements and combined them into one beautiful book to help you anchor in the energy of gratitude:

- ♥ **Stories** – In reading another's story we can relate to and see ourselves in their experience without the pressure to "own" it right then and there. Stories are powerful forces for healing.

- ♥ **Coloring** – Stepping into the power of creativity and color brings another level of healing. When we color, our active mind steps aside, we are present and clear. It truly becomes a meditative and mindfulness practice. Coloring also helps us to move energy that is stuck in the body, which in turn helps us to release that "stuckness."

- ♥ **Journaling** – One of the most powerful ways to really drop into gratitude is through journaling. In fact, when we really commit to journaling (i.e. in *52 Weeks of Gratitude*), we call to us LIFE-CHANGING experiences.

Between the pages of this beautiful book is an array of amazing people willing to share their stories of gratitude with the intention of empowering and enhancing the lives of others. Adding the energy of the coloring pages really cements in your own gratitude in a physical way, which then leads to the journal pages, which allow you to bring it all together in your own heart space. I believe this combination is a perfect way to center in gratitude and truly step into a new practice that can - and will - change your life.

I look forward to crossing paths with you one day, one open grateful heart to another!

In Gratitude and Appreciation,

Sunny Dawn Johnston

SUNNY DAWN JOHNSTON is an acclaimed inspirational speaker, spiritual teacher, and psychic medium. She is the author of twenty books, including her flagship bestsellers, *Invoking the Archangels* and *The Love Never Ends*, which have become the cornerstones for many of her keynote topics such as intuition, mediumship, and the angelic realm.

Through her courses, private sessions, and live events, Sunny has grown and cultivated a diverse global community. Whether in-person or online, her strong mentorship encourages thousands of students to connect with their heart and the core of their being and guides them to experience life in a newer, more positive light.

Sunny is also the creator of the ELEV8 Your Life membership site, a virtual community focused on designing a high-vibrational life bursting with abundance, self-love, and joy. Leading the ELEV8 Your Life community, Sunny focuses on accountability, support, and guidance as the solid foundation of intentional and lasting transformation. To learn more about her work be sure to visit her website.

Connect with Sunny
sunnydawnjohnston.com
ELEV8YourLife.Love

INTRODUCTION

I am delighted you have picked up this journal because that tells me you are ready to create some miracles in your life. Most of us go through short periods (around the holidays, for example) when we feel grateful for what we have; however, when we learn to get into a space of gratitude with regard to all aspects of life, including the challenges, that is where the magic happens. This journal will help you exercise your gratitude "muscle" throughout the entire year. With conscious and consistent practice, gratitude will become a part of the fabric of your life; it will become part of who you are.

This is not just wishful thinking; in fact, there are scientific findings that practicing gratitude every day has positive effects on overall our wellbeing, personally and professionally.

Gratitude improves our:

- ♥ Emotional health. Gratitude strengthens our emotions. We become more resilient. We don't get stuck in the energy of the bad things that happen, but instead learn to hold onto the good memories and let go of the bad. We experience more joy, less envy, and are generally more relaxed.

- ♥ Physical Health. We feel more alive. We have more energy and less stress. We have a better quality of sleep, less physical pain, and even stronger immune systems. This means less trips to the doctor! People who practice gratitude daily simply live longer and happier lives.

- ♥ Social Health. We are friendlier; we cultivate deeper relationships, have better marriages and healthier interactions with family. It has been proven that those who regularly practice gratitude by taking time to notice and reflect upon the things and people they're thankful for experience more positive emotions and express more compassion and kindness. Gratitude makes us nicer, more trustworthy. It helps us to connect with each other more fully and more authentically.

- ♥ Career/business. We have better management skills, increased focus and productivity, better decision-making skills and more efficient networking. We are more likely to reach our goals.

- ♥ Personality. Practicing gratitude makes us more optimistic and less materialistic. We have more self-esteem. It makes us more spiritual and connected to our Source. We will start to see the miracles all around us and see or hear the messages we are supposed to be receiving.

Understand, there is no right or wrong way to practice gratitude; everyone will have a different process. Using this journal as it is intended will positively change your life, I guarantee it. Each week, set aside a small amount of time (thirty minutes to an hour) to read that week's story. Resist the urge to read ahead; just sit with that story and allow it to pull you into the feeling of gratitude expressed by the author. You may even find it inspires you to think about gratitude in a way you never have before. If you'd like, take some time to color the beautiful coloring page, as this will calm and clear your mind as you get ready to journal. Coloring improves your concentration, unleashes your creativity, improves your motor skills, releases negative thoughts, and decreases stress and anxiety. In short, your brain reacts to coloring in the same way it reacts to meditation.

Following each coloring page there is a place for you to journal about what you are grateful for that week. If you would like to take it a step further you could carry this journal (or any notebook) with you, and jot down things as they come to you. Then refer to those notes at the end of the week as you use this journal.

Every night before you go to sleep, think of the positive things that happened during the day. Make practicing gratitude a daily practice with the entire family. At dinner or before bedtime, have everyone in the home express what they are grateful for. Be sure to set the example by expressing your gratitude as well. As you immerse yourself more fully into the energy of gratitude you will not only start to witness the amazing abundance around you, you will open the path for so much more to come to you.

Many blessings on your gratitude journey!

KIM RICHARDSON is a personal chef, health coach, author, and publisher, teaching others how to live in a High Vibrational place of peace, love, and joy. Kim has a real love and passion for food, cooking and teaching how food plays a role in the mind, body, spirit connection.

Through sharing her own personal experiences, she empowers individuals to transform their lives. She helps individuals to heal, forgive and expand without judgment. Her passion is helping people discover their true gifts and how to use them in the world. Kim teaches with unconditional love as she hopes it will have a ripple effect in the world.

Kim resides in Northern Arizona where she enjoys the warm weather and sunshine with her husband, Symon and their fur baby, Hudson.

Connect with Kim
Facebook @ kimrichardson444
YouTube @ goo.gl/8Q5RiW

To learn more about Kim's work and download your free recipe, visit kimrichardson.kim

Week 1

Develop an attitude of gratitude, and give thanks for everything that happens to you, knowing that every step forward is achieving something bigger and better than your current situation.

~ Brian Tracey

GRATITUDE FOR FORGIVENESS

Growing up in an alcoholic family, unpredictability was the norm. We moved frequently, and I attended at least five different elementary schools before I was even in fifth grade. By the time I was nine years old, my parents had divorced, my father had died, and a new stepfather had moved in.

As an adult facing the fact that everyone in my family was an alcoholic, I wrestled with how to handle it. Opening up about my past with close friends, mentors, or my therapist, I always ended the story (if not out loud then at least in my mind) that many others have had it much worse. Describing my mother's parenting style as "benign neglect," I told tales about being a latchkey child, and ranted about all the drunks in our family and even made jokes about all of it. While I made light of my past (probably in an effort to make myself feel better), I was still angry and unable to let it go or forgive. I knew I had been deeply wounded and I knew I wanted to heal.

Reading many books on the matters of healing, self-help and spirituality, helped me tremendously and I moved on to personal healing experiences. Attending a women's retreat weekend where we were to share experiences and role-play with partners, I knew before I left that my work would NOT be about my mother. Of course, Spirit had another idea and my role-playing partner played my mom. The message was clear that I still had work to do.

Shortly after that retreat, I was invited to another gathering of women. We were divided into small groups and assigned to work on a random yet specific topic, to discuss our personal experiences and develop a ceremony around that topic in order to help each other heal. I pulled the topic card for our group from the basket: Forgiveness. Here I go again. Spirit had really turned up the volume, just in case I wasn't getting it.

Not much later, I was invited to attend another workshop called "Radical Forgiveness," in which of course I participated and let go of more layers of old wounds. In another women's circle, we were asked to work on our "mother issues" and to begin by writing her story as objectively as we could. I scoffed at the idea. How could I write HER story? I was still too invested in MY story. I put off writing it until the night before our meeting. It was eye-opening to try to see the world from her point of view. More layers of healing occurred.

During my studies to become a shamanic practitioner, I burned, buried and released all kinds of symbolic things in order to forgive my parents, especially my mom. These events and many others all happened within a few years. Spirit was guiding, I have no doubt. I never ran away from doing healing work, but still could not seem to get to a point where I felt fully "there," truly healed and whole. Though each of these workshops, retreats and ceremonies provided me with baby steps toward forgiveness, I never quite released all the anger and resentment I felt at not having had a "normal" childhood. Envious of friends who had healthy and happy families, I now worried about how my past and my outlook on life affected my own children.

After each healing experience, I felt somewhat better, yet seemed to always sink back into a mode of "why me." I hated feeling like a victim. I sometimes berated myself for these feelings, telling myself, again, that it wasn't so bad. I wasn't abused physically. My mom was a really nice person, she was fun, she loved nature like me, and on and on. But as I learned in therapy, you cannot deny your feelings, and your story is your own story. If we compare our story to others or diminish it, we are not honoring our own. I wanted to honor my story and I wanted to change it going forward.

Then my mother got cancer. For three short months, I watched her fight. During my flights back and forth to Phoenix, I saw her lying there in the hospital bed with all the tubes and medical paraphernalia helping her to hang on. And I began to really see HER, not what she was in the past, but her true essence.

It is so hard to explain in words, yet I must try. When I walked in her room, I saw only her pure spirit lying in the bed, as if there was no body. I saw and felt her soul, her spirit. My body and heart began to soften. In those times, we were connecting soul to soul, not mother with daughter. In those moments, I found it was difficult NOT to forgive.

Initially after her death, it surprised me that I felt relief and then I felt guilty for that. I had been starved for a mother-daughter relationship and now no longer had to crave it. My ego was no longer tied to her beliefs, judgments, or lack of caring of what I was doing. My own negative judgements of my mother gradually dissipated. As I let go of that, I felt a freedom to be who I truly am.

All the workshops and practices that I had experienced culminated into a heart-opening space and connected me to my own spirit and essence. Slowly the little girl in me, the one that was not given much love and carried these deep wounds, came forth. She came to me in dreams and through journaling and in a women's circle, and she spoke to me. She told me I needed to be seen and heard, and visible. I welcomed her as she taught me to love myself, for exactly who I am. This is what I had needed all along.

My lessons rapidly escalated. A deep integration has taken place since my mother's death thirteen years ago. Through doing my own inner work and now being a women's circle facilitator, I have learned so much. We always are learning. What I know for sure: If we become trapped by our conditions and blame everyone else, we can never grow. Until we acknowledge and accept our feelings, we cannot move forward. Until we choose to stop living our lives in a victim role, we cannot be free. Until we consciously and intentionally let go of our judgments, we cannot love ourselves or others.

I asked myself: If I didn't have this story, then what was my story? Who would I be? I was exhausted from telling that same old story. Our perceptions of our life are just that – perceptions. We can change our perceptions.

The story may be words to describe my life, but it is not who I AM. The purpose of life is to honor the lessons we receive, learn from them, and become more loving humans. As I honor my own past, I honor my mother's life and the myriad challenges she experienced. I am grateful to accept and forgive. Finally, I am able to realize deep and true radical forgiveness, for her and for myself. My gratitude today and every day is for that forgiveness. My life is now filled with gratitude for this path of compassion and self-love that brings me, at long last, sweet peace.

CHRISTINE MOSES MS, Founder of Featherheart Holistic Paths, provides counseling and guidance for personal and spiritual growth as well as the facilitation of women's groups and retreats for integration of mind, body and spirit. As a long-time student and apprentice of cross-cultural traditions and nature-based spirituality, her offerings include many healing traditions. Bridging traditional psychology and intuitive tools with Native American spirituality and healing practices, she supports clients on their journey through transformational work with sacredness and compassion.

Christine holds a Master of Science in Holistic Ministries, is a certified Shamanic Practitioner, Reiki Master, Ordained Interfaith Minister, Ceremonialist, Certified Retreat Leader and author.

Additionally, she trains other women to lead sacred circles. Her book The Wisdom of Circles: Gathering Women for Conscious Community is a combination of her personal journey and healing story, a training guide, and an empowering inspiration.

Connect with Christine
chrisfeatherheart.com
christinemoses11@gmail.com
847-525-2600

I am grateful for ...

_____
_____
_____
_____
_____
_____
_____
_____
_____
_____
_____
_____
_____
_____
_____
_____
_____
_____
_____
_____
_____
_____
_____
_____
_____
_____
_____
_____
_____
_____
_____
_____
_____
_____
_____
_____
_____
_____
_____

Week 2

*At times, our own light goes out and is kindled by a spark
from another person. Each of us has cause to think
with deep gratitude of those who have lighted the flame within us.*

~ Albert Schweitzer

BE THE CHANGE YOU WANT TO SEE

One moment I was enjoying the wind rush through my hair, the next moment, I was shaking hands with the grim reaper in a roadside ditch! I was seventeen years old and had been in a motorcycle accident that nearly cost me my life and in many ways it did. As I experienced the physical and mental challenges and torment that followed, I realized many things that I otherwise would have never known. This was a turning point in my life that defined me for many years. I was a victim. Then I was a survivor. Now, I am grateful!

Gratitude did not come about in a day or a moment. It was a process. There have been many ups and downs, valleys, peaks, and cycles on my road to gratitude. There is no one size fits all. One must discover their own path and recognize their journey. Every living being will experience adverse conditions without end, but suffering is optional. The key to enduring and transforming these moments is to acknowledge the lesson. Ignoring or covering up the circumstance does not make it go away. Instead, deliberately transform these negative emotions and adversity into virtue that benefits yourself and others. Without this transformation, the suffering will continue to grow. We tend to feed the negative. Consider feeding the positive and fill your mind with gratitude, compassion, and love. This is practice, not perfection. It is a simple concept, but it is not easy.

Why did I suffer a life-threatening head injury so early in life, followed by chronic rare health conditions? To learn patience and empathy. When I awoke the five-day comma, I had to relearn basic faculties such as walking and feeding myself. I woke up without memory of my childhood and had to piece my life back together. It was like Humpty Dumpty falling off the wall. Only I was the only one who could see I was broken. This made it very easy to be a victim of the accident. I was told that I changed and that I was not the person I was before the accident. It seems that all those around me liked the person I was before, but I did not know who that was or how to become that again. I suffered global brain damage, but the majority of the injury was to my frontal lobe that controls memory and emotions. I felt nothing and had to relearn how to recognize and identify emotions. I wanted so badly to be what others remembered. I felt all alone in a world of friends that didn't understand. They were teenagers just like me, however, they had their memory. As I grew older, I developed chronic rare health conditions. They are linked to my endocrine system not functioning properly due to the damage suffered. I now depend on synthetic hormones to keep me in balance. Why does all of this matter? Because these adverse conditions are not going away but it is my choice if I suffer. I have increased my empathy of those who are inflicted with physical limitations and chronic conditions. I am patient with myself and others because I know how it feels to be controlled and limited by my body.

Why did my friends walk away from me in my time of need? So that I could learn forgiveness. There were many years that I fled the scene and did my best to disappear and leave the place where people knew my name. I wanted to create my own identity and not be compared to that girl that I was before the accident. This led to a series of depression, substance abuse, running away, mania, and many other mental conditions. Fortunately, I have a wonderful family that kept me grounded and I was able to return to a place of love and understanding. I thought that if I just acted like it never happened then it would all go away. I could go on functioning like everyone else. I masked the pain in many ways. I worked 80 plus hours a week. I was a functioning alcoholic. I focused on my outward appearance so that no one would want to know what was behind the personal walls I had built up to protect me from feeling the hurt. Eventually I sorted out that I was hiding. I chose to forgive and love those who hurt me. The weight of the world lifted, and I felt a freedom I never knew.

Why did I experience abusive relationships? So that I could learn strength and confidence. I allowed myself to be in harm's way and was attracted to those who use others to feel superior. I believed that I was inferior and damaged. It led me down a path of destruction. When I realized how far down the rabbit hole I had ventured. I took appropriate actions to find my way out. I realized that I had the strength and wisdom to stand on my own. I am worthy. I am abundant. I am love. With this new strength and confidence, I walked away and wished them well in their journey.

May everyone be happy,
May everyone be free from misery,
May no one ever be separated from their happiness,
May everyone have equanimity, free from hatred and attachment.
~Geshe Kelsang Gyatso

There is an abundant supply of adversity and we all experience it. Be grateful for it. The conditions we experience allow us to grow and practice love. Authentic love, without conditions. Personally, I noticed a shift in me when I learned to stop comparing my suffering and success to others. My suffering is not more or less than the next person and neither is my success. It is not about having more material things or a larger bank account or better physical form or even that my suffering is greater or less than the suffering of others. Do what makes you happy, be with who makes you smile, laugh as much as you breathe, love as long as you live. The opinion of others does not define you. Focus on being a better you than you were the day before. No need for it to be in the front of your mind at all time, just recognize how you improved, regardless of how little, and be grateful that you were blessed with the opportunity to flourish. At the end of the day be happy that you connected with the cashier at the grocery, you assisted an elderly woman get to her car, completed 10,000 steps, didn't eat the whole pint of ice cream, or called a friend you have not spoken with for a few months.

There is a voice inside of you that whispers all day long ...'I feel that this is right for me; I know that this is wrong.' No teacher, preacher, parent, friend or wise man can decide what's right for you – just listen to the voice that speaks inside.

~Shel Silverstein

Be careful not to criticize when doing this. Stop using words like miserable, jealous, angry, drained, and stressed. The more you say them, the more you focus on, believe, create, and feel it. Stop telling others and reinforcing negative situations and emotions. Start saying I am okay, I can, I will, I am ...! You will begin to feel better mentally and physically! I AM ... two of the most powerful words; for what you put after them shapes your reality. Marinate with this and program your subconscious mind. The currency of life is your positive thoughts in order to create your desires and put them into motion. I was told that I would be fortunate to graduate high school and would never be able to get a college education due to the limitations of my brain caused by the injury. However, my mind had other plans. It was difficult and challenging but I graduated high school with honors and completed a bachelor's degree. It took many additional hours and dedication. But I chose perseverance. I chose success without boundaries.

The best way to dispel a negative thought is to require that it has a purpose. Consider filling your mind with gratitude for all experiences, as they allow compassion and understanding of the world. It does not have to be perfect. Be grateful and enjoy the messy, imperfect, and beautiful journey of life.

KATINA GILLESPIE FERRELL a bestselling author, client project manager, and practicing Buddhist. She has experienced countless phases where she reinvented herself while connecting with her inner knowing and following the wisdom of her wild heart. The circumstances that surround her have developed unwavering love and compassion for others with a desire to end suffering and allow happiness for all living beings. Each morning when I open my eyes, I say to myself "I, not events, have the power to make me happy or unhappy."

Connect with Katina

Facebook @ emotionalharmonywellness

I am grateful for ...

Week 3

Gratitude turns what we have into enough.

~ Anonymous

GRACE + ATTITUDE = GRATITUDE

What is gratefulness? The dictionary definition says: appreciation of benefits received; expressing gratitude; being grateful; thankfulness. The definition really doesn't do the word any justice at all.

The law of attraction says that we manifest into our lives whatever we focus on. Since the law of attraction doesn't have the ability to discern, we are equally capable of attracting what we don't want as we are our heart's desires. If we focus on gratitude, we will bring more things into our lives to be grateful for. It really makes me wonder how we get from knowing what gratitude is, to embodying it.

Many of us need to be taught how to be grateful, how to appreciate the things we have—the friends and family we are surrounded by, and who we are. Some of us are grateful to others for everything and do not appreciate or show gratitude to ourselves. And then there are those of us who are afraid to ask for anything from anyone and have a difficult time accepting any thanks or appreciation that is aimed at us. There have also been times when I felt gratitude and failed to share it, times remembered with a sense of regret. Since then I have vowed not to take those opportunities for granted.

I am a yoga instructor, and at the end of class, I routinely ask my students to give themselves thanks for showing up to yoga practice, to show themselves gratitude. Some of my students have told me that they really don't know what to do with that statement. Being able to give ourselves that sense of thankfulness and acceptance is essential. Without realizing it, those students who show up in my yoga class are actively expressing self-love and gratefulness for the practice. These simple acts embody and express gratitude. Over the years I have seen and felt the results of showing gratefulness toward others in thought and action, even when it was difficult.

When I taught elementary school, I had a troubled 5th-grade boy in my class one year. Although we got along well enough, there were challenges along the way. Most of the time when I asked him a question, he would refuse to answer. Not once was I able to have him finish a test without either an emotional breakdown or a silent refusal to complete the test. I cared a great deal about him and was concerned about his future. I let him know this, but he never responded when I talked to him about it. Toward the end of the school year, his mother asked me if I thought he should be schooled differently for the upcoming year (6th grade ... yikes). I recommended she consider alternatives to a regular school. The following year I didn't see him at school and often wondered about him. Fast-forward four years; it was my last day before retiring from elementary school teaching. This former student of mine had heard that I was retiring and showed up to wish me well. I couldn't believe it was the same boy. He thanked me and told me that those small gestures meant a great deal to him, even though he wasn't able to express it at the time. I'm grateful to this young man for showing me that positive gestures, thoughts, and feelings do matter and have an impact in ways we may never know.

We do not always get to see how the gratitude we've shown others impacts their lives, but we know how showing or not showing gratitude impacts our own lives. It matters, even if no one else knows.

How can we show gratefulness? It can be as simple as a smile that lets someone know you are happy to see them, or it can be something tangible—a gift or thank you card, or it can be spending time with someone.

Adopting a daily practice of gratitude manifests more things into your life to be grateful for. Each night as I lay my head down to sleep, I send positive thoughts and blessings to my children and loved ones. I also bring to mind something that I feel positive about. Doing this has provided me with a beautiful sense of gratefulness. I do the same thing each morning upon awakening. (It's usually my coffee I'm thankful for; that's okay, right?) Following this practice, evening and morning, helps me to stay present, positive, and appreciative of all the blessings that are available to me. It doesn't mean life is perfect; it just means that I recognize the positive things more than any negative things.

Personally, gratitude (I think of it as grace and attitude) allows me to focus on the details of why I feel content; it's that positive feeling of being part of something larger than myself. I'm humbled but at the same time know that the positive energy I bring by being grateful benefits all.

Gratitude isn't something that we can hold in our hands; it's something that we have in our hearts and share with others every chance we get.

GINA E. MCELROY is a retired elementary school teacher and a current online English teacher. She has her own yoga business where she specializes in private yoga instruction. Since teaching and yoga are two of her passions, she has combined them and works for a yoga studio where she teaches all ages and manages a kid's yoga program.

Gina is a lifelong learner and is continuing her education in advanced yoga teacher training and is a certified Mindfulness and Guided Imagery Facilitator. Grateful for all of her blessings, Gina gives back to the community by overseeing and teaching yoga and meditation for kids and adults at a local domestic violence shelter.

Connect with Gina
Facebook @ gina.mcelroy.547

I am grateful for ...

Week 4

*Gratitude is not only the greatest
Of all virtues, but the parent of all others.*

~ Marcus Tullius Cicero

HOW GRATITUDE HELPED ME HEAL MY LIFE

In August of 2011, I was diagnosed with stage three peritoneal cancer. I was angry, and I was scared. I didn't know what to do. After the initial shock wore off, and after two surgeries and chemotherapy, I recognized that something had to change. I realized that I had to shift the way I looked at things, and to be grateful for everything. That is exactly what I did. I started with a small gratitude practice by counting one or two things to be grateful for each day. Before I knew it, I felt a big shift. Life was good, regardless of the dreadful diagnosis and regardless of the uncertain journey that lay ahead. I knew I wanted more Life.

Life is a series of lessons to learn, grow, and heal from, and those lessons expand your soul. Life goes by quickly. When you are grateful for the lessons from your life experiences and are able to let go of any pain, shame, or guilt that has kept you stuck, then you are able to shine brightly.

When we give cheerfully and accept gratefully, everyone is blessed
~ Maya Angelou

I have learned that the greatest prayer is Thank You and that this prayer alone attracts to us wonderful opportunities, people, places, and things. Gratitude recognizes the good in life. Be thankful for what you already have and the Universe ushers in more to be grateful for. Be thankful for your life. Every day is a blessing, so focus on what you already have and not on what you don't have. Energy flows where your attention goes, so keep those thoughts in a gratitude vibration.

Open yourself up to gratitude and develop an attitude of gratitude by setting an intention to be grateful each and every day.

Gratitude turns what we have into enough and opens the door to more. It boosts emotional well-being and helps your mind, body, and spirit by enhancing your life with feel-good endorphins. Gratitude truly is the best attitude.

I begin each day by giving thanks. I thank God for my life, my body, my family, and the day. I also ask how I may be of service, then I open my arms to receive all the blessings the Universe has in store for me.
When you stay in a gratitude vibration you align your vibration with the blessings waiting to come to you. Have faith that it is on its way and trust in the Divine timing. Follow your guidance and then take any inspired action to manifest all your dreams, desires, wishes, and goals.

Commit time each day to your new practice. This will create a healthy new habit. The more you practice gratitude the more it will become a wonderful habit that is filled with faith, magic, and miracles.

To help you practice gratitude daily and to begin each day with a grateful heart, here are ways to bring more positivity into your life.

- ♥ Start a gratitude journal or jar and add to it each day
- ♥ Practice kindness by performing random acts of kindness as this balances your energy of giving and receiving
- ♥ Love yourself first
- ♥ Appreciate everything as appreciation appreciates
- ♥ Find the value in your lessons and find the positive in your experiences
- ♥ Spend more time with loved ones
- ♥ Smile often
- ♥ Add love when you cook
- ♥ Notice the beauty of and in nature
- ♥ Stop complaining
- ♥ Live mindfully by staying present in each day. The past is gone so forget it. The future isn't here yet so don't worry.
- ♥ Forgive
- ♥ Bless yourself, your life, your job, your family, your friends, God, your food, your water. Bless everything.
- ♥ Pray or meditate. Give thanks to our Creator, as the prayer THANK YOU is very powerful.

The more you thank Life, the more that Life will give you to be thankful for.

Gratitude Prayer

Dear Universe,

Today and every day

I will find things to be grateful for.

I will say thank you from an open heart.

I will be open to receiving my blessings and I will smile because

Life is so good! Thank you for my beautiful life and for our beautiful world.

Thank you for helping me along my journey to have the strength and courage to change the things I can and for the wisdom to know when I cannot.

Thank you for all my blessings and for the ones yet to come.

Amen and so it is.

Wear gratitude like a cloak and it will feed every corner of your life…

~ Rumi

Gratitude Affirmations:

Thank you, God, for this day

Thank you for all my blessings

I am grateful

I am grateful for all my abundance

Thank you for my life

I will be thankful for all life brings to me

Every day there is something to appreciate

I express my faith with gratitude for all there is

I am blessed

I am Divine

I have within me a deep wisdom to help me get through all life lessons

My heart is filled with love

I am thankful for simply being alive today

GIULIANA MELO believes in the Divine healing energy of the Universe with her entire being. She loves being of service and connecting others to their angels. She is a fun and faithful angel intuitive who is shining her light and loving life!

Having walked her own journey of cancer and grief, she now supports others through their life struggles with help from God and the angelic realm through angel card readings and angel prayers.

If you are looking for someone who exudes love and makes you feel special and loved, then look no further. She will guide and support you with; love, support, and connection to your Divine Team.

If you have been feeling called to get to know your guardian angels or tap into your intuitive gifts, then contact her.

Connect with Giuliana
giulianamelo.com
jmelo10@shaw.ca
Facebook @ healwithgiulianamelo

I am grateful for ...

Week 5

When you truly feel into, and embrace gratitude-it changes your life by opening a doorway to an endless supply of things to be grateful for.

~ Janice Story

EMBRACING GRATITUDE

I have so much to be grateful for in my life: a loving family, dear friends, pets, a roof over my head, and food on the table. For most people, these are the main ingredients of life, the things that if asked, they would say they are very grateful for. Of course, each of us also has our own stories of survival, trauma, and challenges that we've overcome, which in turn has given us even more reasons to be thankful. But how often do we take the time to express gratitude for the little things we are blessed with in the day-to-day?

To be honest, I've always felt truly thankful for all I have been gifted with, despite - or perhaps, because - I had endured, physical, emotional and sexual abuse, as well as a horrific car accident. But a few years back I realized something was missing. I didn't really know how to love myself or receive that love from others. When someone gave me a compliment or a gift, I would smile and say thank you - and while I truly meant it, I also had a hard time allowing myself to actually feel grateful because subconsciously I did not feel worthy or deserving of their kindness. I wanted to be the giver; I wanted to make others happy. It would take me some time and a lot of inner work before I was able to let my walls down and learn, not only to love myself, but to allow myself to receive from others.

Once I began allowing myself to deeply feel and embrace gratitude, an amazing shift happened. I started experiencing more joy and happiness, and as I did many other wonderful things started showing up for me. As my own gratitude grew, I was increasingly enabled to share that gratitude with and be of service to others. There have been so many tools that have helped me, but I'd like to share with you a few of the most powerful that taught me to fully embrace gratitude.

Keep a Journal. Many people recognize journaling as a way of releasing negativity, but it can also be a great way to express the good things. Start writing out a daily message of what you are grateful for: events, people, experiences, et cetera. Visualize them and feel the emotions of love and gratitude. Allow yourself to relive the experiences as you write. For example, if you are writing about your son, let your body feel like it did the very first time you held him. If it's your wedding day, remember what the flowers smelled like, or what it felt like as you walked down the aisle in your dress.

Change your Perspective. Take a challenging experience and look for something positive that came from it. For example, I am grateful for the hard lessons and traumatic events that I've had I'm my life. I've learned from them, and now I am being guided to be of help and support to others.

Share the Attitude of Gratitude. Reach out to someone via text, email, snail mail or phone and let them know how grateful you are to have them in your life. Sharing your gratitude with others creates and attracts more gratitude for everyone.

Stop and smell the roses. This is much more than an empty platitude; in fact, enjoyment of the natural world is one of the fastest and most profound ways we have to experience gratitude. Sit out in nature and feel the earth under your feet. Listen to the wind whistling through the trees, the sounds of the birds chirping. Hear the rustling of the critters in the brush. Enjoy the smells from the flowers or the fresh cut grass. Feel the warmth of the sun on your face. Remember when you were a child - the joy of jumping in the mud puddles or trying to catch snowflakes on your tongue. As we get older, we get so busy sometimes that we forget how grateful we are for all of the beauty that surrounds us. Now is the time to slow down, remember and re-immerse ourselves in it!

Use Gratitude with the Law of Attraction. Gratitude is a highly effective tool for manifesting our heart's desires. Journal about what you want as if you've already received it. Write out your wishes on sticky notes to place everywhere as affirmations. These are just a few ideas, so don't be afraid to get creative! For example, write in your journal, "I am so grateful for my new job that I just love!" or "I am grateful for the ten clients that I have seen this week!" Jot down on sticky notes, "I am grateful that my house has sold," or "I am grateful for my new truck," et cetera. Live it, think it, feel it, and believe it like you already have it, then watch the magic happen! Meditating on and journaling about my gratitude has empowered me and expanded my life in countless ways, and it will do the same for you.

I am so grateful for all of the amazing friendships I have made, and the support and help they have given me on my journey. I'm thankful for all of the life lessons I have been given – even (and perhaps especially) the most difficult ones. I hope you have an amazing experience embracing your own gratitude, as you journal your way through this book. Enjoy your journey, my friends!

JANICE STORY is a gifted Certified Reiki Master Teacher who from an early age experienced a tremendous amount of trauma. As Janice moved through her own healing, she uncovered the value of her suffering and decided to channel these experiences into a source of healing for others.

Working from a beautiful sanctuary in her home, she provides safety for her clients as they learn to feel, release and embrace their own journeys. Janice also brings her horses, with whom she has always had a strong connection, into her work. She hosts workshops and trainings where she and these majestic animals help create an opening for healing and transformation in ways beyond that of human contact alone.

Connect with Janice
janicestory.com
janice.story@me.com

I am grateful for ...

Week 6

Gratitude unlocks the fullness of life. It turns what we have into enough, and more. It turns denial into acceptance, chaos to order, confusion to clarity. It can turn a meal into a feast, a house into a home, a stranger into a friend.

~ Melody Beattie

GRATITUDE IS ALL THERE IS

Merriam-Webster's definition of Gratitude is: the state of being grateful. Expresses gratitude for their support.

Dictionary.com's definition of gratitude is: the quality or feeling of being grateful or thankful.

The British Dictionary's definition is: a feeling of thankfulness or appreciation, as for gifts or favors.

The commonality of each of these definitions is that being grateful is a feeling or a quality of being.

I was not brought up learning how to be grateful. I was taught impeccable manners, and the difference between right and wrong, but not the art of gratitude. I feel that by not learning to be thankful or grateful about what I had was a true disservice to the betterment of my life.

For decades, I would go through the motions of thanking those who had given me

material gifts or who had done something for me, but I really didn't know how to feel grateful, that is until I started down my spiritual path. I learned as I began my journey how being grateful for absolutely everything that I experienced in my life, is something to be thankful for.

At first it was hard for me to wrap my mind around being grateful for a broken heart or to not get something that you thought you really wanted, or from the plethora of places where we feel lack or of not being enough. I didn't understand what there was to be grateful for when I felt, angry, hurt or depressed about a situation or myself.

When I looked back at the situations that I was so affected by, I realized that if I would have gotten that job, or relationship, or any of the millions of things I thought I wanted, that it would have hindered me and/or my personal, spiritual, and/or emotional growth. In other words, I dodged a lot of bullets by not getting what thought I had wanted in those moments. I also expended a lot of energy in the wrong places and often lost focus.

I'm happy to share that my life and its current ebb and flow is a one-hundred-and-eighty-degree difference from how it started. I am joyful and am able to live a life that is led from my heart. I am able to be more accepting of the things that come into my life that I don't believe I wanted, because I know that once I investigate what it is I'm supposed to get from the experience, I will then understand that it's for not only my best and highest good, but for the highest good for all involved.

I want to share with you my gratitude practice. I start my day with prayer. I begin my prayers by announcing to Spirit: "I greet you this day with Love, Joy and with Gratitude". I continue by declaring what I am grateful for. This includes the people, my pets, the places I am able to go to and things have and that I love and appreciate. I always add how I am grateful for absolutely everything that I have experienced in my life up until that very moment. I add into this portion of thankfulness that I'm not only grateful for the positive events, people thoughts or things I've experienced in my life, but I'm also grateful for the "perceived" negative things and experiences that I have encountered. I then acknowledge that I know that those "perceived" negative things were a lesson, opportunity, a gift or a combination of them all.

I also end my day, as I close my eyes by thanking Spirit for everything that I had experienced or came encountered. My husband tells me when I fall asleep, that there's a little smile on my face.

I invite you to begin a gratitude practice and to see your life shift before your eyes. You don't have to do it the way I do, because a practice is as personal of act as one may have. Try different ways to incorporate gratitude into your day. It can easily be done while in front of the mirror as you get ready to start your day, or while driving, or while cooking.

I think you understand what I'm saying. It's your life and only you walk in your shoes. You might be thinking to yourself what can I be grateful or thankful for? Start small, start by being thankful you woke up and can experience a new day. You can be grateful you have a toothbrush and toothpaste, or toilet paper, hot water, or you can be grateful for your job, even if you hate what you're doing, knowing that it brings you income to eat, pay bills, shop and have the things you want. I'm confident that you will start to identify not only big things in your life, but you'll start to notice small things that in the past might have seemed inconsequential.

To see how being grateful is a vehicle to happy, joyful, blissful change, try documenting how you feel when you wake up and how you feel before bed. There will be days where you may say phooey, but then when you look back on your writings, you will see how this wonderful emotion will eek into your being.

MARLA GOLDBERG is a Healer, Intuitive, Speaker, Author and Host of Guided Spirit Conversations podcast. Marla's mission is to help people by Inspiring, Motivating, and Educating them giving them insights, tools and techniques that will help them shift or enhance their current life circumstances.

Marla has been trained in over twenty healing and clearing modalities and has been walking this magical path for over fifteen years, bridging together her intuitive abilities with the modalities she works on with her clients. Successfully assisting her clients in transforming their lives. When not working, Marla enjoys traveling, painting, yoga, meditation, or exploring life's curiosities. She also shares her life with her husband Gary and her two loving pet companions; Mabel and Tug.

Connect with Marla
mghealer.com
marla@mghealer.com

I am grateful for ...

Week 7

*Feeling gratitude and not expressing it, is
like wrapping a present and not giving it.*

~ William Arthur Ward

MINNETTE'S TRANSITION

One grey winter Sunday we visited my husband's mom, Minnette, at her Assisted Living Center.

It was going to be a tough visit; she was in the end stages of Alzheimer's. She hadn't been eating for a week and was interested only in ice chips or water. We were advised by her Doctor not to force any food. He suggested that we, however difficult it was, accept that this was her choice and it was common at this stage in the patients with this disease.

She had moments of clarity, which we were so grateful for. At one point early on in our visit my husband sat close to her on her sofa and putting his head on her shoulder he said, "Am I still your favorite son?" She said, "You're my only son." We all smiled.

We listened to the Frank Sinatra CDs that we brought for her and watched her tap her toes. I brought my angel cards too, knowing how she liked to play cards. I asked her if she would like to pick three and I would give her a reading. After all, I thought, if the cards are all about energy not intellect, then a reading is still possible. I had remembered reading something about looking at a rock under a special microscope and it showed only movement, and vibration.

I knocked the old energy out of the cards and shuffled them three times spreading them out as I was advised in my Certification course. I asked her to choose three cards, one at a time and she seemed happy to pick her cards.

Before she chose her cards, I said a little prayer as I always do, that the reading be for her highest and best. I started to lose her when I began explaining the process and decided I must keep it simple. "It's okay," I told her. "Just think about whatever you'd like, and the Angels will deliver the message that is your own."

She chose the first card and the second, then the third. They were carefully chosen and then she passed the cards to me. They felt like a beautifully wrapped gift. All three cards would be connected. If the wisdom in the first card resonated, the advice in the second card would follow and so on with the third card. We would be surprised at what was about to be revealed from the Divine realm.

The first card was Acceptance. It read: "I am in complete acceptance of my current situation. All is in right action on my path." The relief on my husband's face was worth diamonds.

The second card was Sobriety. At first this was difficult to understand because she wasn't even drinker when she was healthy. The meaning in Angel cards is not always literal but metaphorical. With my sister-in-law's help we figured out that it was about a purification process. Minnette's choosing to not eat was a way to purify herself before her transition. More relief went around the room.

The third card was Divine Timing. This card was about everything being in perfect timing on her journey and again reiterated complete acceptance. What a gift the angels had given to us, to those who loved her and worried when she wasn't eating or was not herself, ravaged by this disease.

These cards she carefully chose aligned with her energy to share her state of being. As jumbled as her mind could be at times, this experience clearly taught us that her essence, was a higher energy than her thought pattern.

She along with her higher angels, were guiding us, and what a relief to truly know she was cradled in the everlasting love of the Divine.

Although we were grieving our loss of Minnette already, we left that day filled with gratitude for her and the guidance that came through so loud and clear to tell us she was perfectly safe and cared for all along.

ROSEMARY HURWITZ, a married mom of four young adults, is passionate about an inner-directed life and she found the focus for it in the Enneagram. The Enneagram is a time-honored personality to higher consciousness paradigm used worldwide. She received her Enneagram Certification in an MA. Pastoral Studies program at Loyola University, Chicago, in 2001. Rosemary has studied and taught the Enneagram ever since. She also gives Enneagram-based individual coaching for self-awareness and emotional wellness.

Rosemary has a BA in Broadcast Communication, and Certifications in Intuitive Counseling and Angel Card Reading and uses these wisdom traditions in her spiritual teaching and coaching. For over twenty years, along with her husband, she gave Discovery Weekend retreats, patterned after Marriage Encounter, for engaged couples. She is a Professional member of the International Enneagram Association. Reviews at spiritdrivenliving.com.

This is Rosemary's fifth co-authored inspirational book, and *Who You Are Meant to Be: The Enneagram Effect,* her first single-authored book is coming soon!

Connect with Rosemary
rosepetalmusic@gmail.com
spiritdrivenliving.com

I am grateful for ...

Week 8

Imperfection is beauty, madness is genius and it's better to be absolutely ridiculous than absolutely boring.

~ Marilyn Monroe

INFINITE UNCONDITIONAL LOVE

The day I was told I was pregnant with my second child Ciara was the beginning of my gratitude journey. It was also the start of a journey of two souls fulfilling their purpose together.

I wasn't always grateful for this journey; in fact, I exhausted a lot of energy feeling sorry for myself. As parents we all face different challenges, none more or less important than someone else's, yet it can sometimes feel as though we've been handed the worst lot in the world. Like all of our experiences while wearing this "suit of flesh," these challenges have been chosen by our own spirit to teach us whatever it is we need to learn in this particular lifetime. Oftentimes, as in the case with me and my precious daughter, our souls join with others so that we can learn together and teach each other.

When she was nine months old Ciara was diagnosed with hypotonia and ataxia, neurodevelopmental disorders with a host of symptoms that include spasms and delays in speech and other milestones. And that was just the beginning. Next came the possibility of cerebral palsy – which is often associated with her conditions - then her eating disorder due to her allergies, and the breathing treatments that had to be administered four times each day. And, as if that wasn't enough, on the week of her second birthday her father decided to exit her life, leaving me to love and care, not only for Ciara, but for her older brother, Bo. How was I to do this? I was so consumed with the task before me that the thought of loving and caring for myself never entered my mind.

We did receive some relatively good news later that month. Ciara was diagnosed, not with cerebral palsy, but with pervasive developmental disorder. Though this was a less severe condition, it nevertheless required multiple therapies each week and seemingly endless doctor appointments. This, coupled with the fact that we lived in a rural area, made it difficult to provide for my children. At this point in time there was not a mustard seed of gratitude in my soul. I was scared, frustrated, and totally pissed that God had handed us this horrific life. Between doctor appointments and therapy for Ciara; t-ball, soccer, and Boy Scouts for Bo; church services, teaching Sunday School, choir practice; and - oh wait, my job! - I was mentally and physically exhausted.

Six months later, the picture started to look a little brighter, and I started to find gratitude. My children and I were able to relocate to Phoenix, thanks to financial assistance from my mother. Just as we were starting this new chapter, however, Ciara received the diagnosis of autism, a neurodevelopmental disorder that affects speech, fine motor functions, sensory input, and social interactions. Ciara is on the severe end of the autism spectrum, meaning she needs 24/7 care. She is non-communicative. She also has sensory integration disorder and craves different tactile sensations for her hands and mouth. She has an extreme sensitivity to noisy public places and events. With that diagnosis came yet another new way of life, another steep learning curve. However, in seeking out the knowledge of what would help Ciara, I discovered my new career. When I realized compression therapy calmed her nervous system, my higher self guided me to massage school. I got my first massage job as soon as I graduated, and within a year's time I owned my own spa with people working for me.

We were still not on easy street, but that little mustard seed of gratitude was beginning to sprout. Truth be told, the toughest experience hadn't yet reared its ugly head. And when it did, I found myself back on "empty," filled with blame and anger and completely devoid of gratitude. Ciara began having self-injurious behaviors (SIBs). She pulled her hair out by handfuls until she had bald spots. She would bite herself hard, tearing into her flesh, and bit me as well when I tried to restrain her. She would hit herself in the face and head so fiercely she would end up with horrific bruises. These behaviors, I learned, are her way of expressing pain; however, since she didn't speak, it seemed hopeless to figure out what the cause was.

What followed were more doctors, more disappointment and more anger – it seemed never-ending. Ciara was diagnosed with eosinophilic esophagitis (EOE), a chronic inflammatory disease related to allergies. It is also extremely painful. To date there is no cure, just a recommendation to be mindful of her diet.

Though my own already trickling creek of gratitude had completely dried up, I remained in awe of this mighty little girl and devout in showing her the unconditional love she deserves. These days, I try to be mindful with hope and knowing that just as the universe replenishes the creek in the woods with snow and rain, she will somehow replenish our creek to flow and be cleansed, all in divine time.

Why do I tell this story? To let you know that like a creek, gratitude ebbs and flows. Even the most positive person has their moments of despair, so don't beat yourself up if you don't have grateful eyes or a fully grateful heart one hundred percent of the time. Shit happens.

When you're feeling overwhelmed by life, stop, take a few deep breaths, scream, cry, and then just pick up your crown again. Yes, I said AGAIN; when you are once again ready to proceed and overflow with gratitude and unconditional love. There is always a chance to recover and move on, and for that, I am most grateful. So join me in giving ourselves a hug of unconditional love and gratitude –because we deserve it!

CASANDRA ELTZROTH is a bad-ass mom, successful massage therapist, empath, craniosacral therapist, reiki practitioner, and spa owner, facilitating and embracing the essence of healing to those called to receive.

She was born in Fort Payne, Alabama, and now resides in Phoenix, Arizona. Casandra has acknowledged her fears and moves forward with grace, ease, and courage, pacing herself so that she has energy to support herself, her relationships, her projects, and two amazing children. Even she doesn't know how she does so much with so little time, but she rests in the knowledge that anything can be achieved in divine timing and with infinite unconditional love.

Connect with Casandra
Facebook @ casandra.eltzroth888
Casandra_srt@yahoo.com

I am grateful for ...

Week 9

As we express our gratitude, we must never forget that the highest appreciation is not to utter words, but to live by them.

~ John F. Kennedy

YOU ARE LOVED

When I was 8 years old, I witnessed my younger nephew (yes, nephew) get run over by a car and critically injured. Ever since that day, any scene which reminded my psyche of that moment would have me scream and run the other way. The emotional encoding of that experience was not a good thing, especially if someone needed my help. Every time I witnessed my children get hurt, my knee jerk reaction was to RUN AWAY. As a mother I needed to learn to disarm this encoding so that I could be present with my children.

Later in life, my career choice positioned me in a role where I created, trained and implemented emergency protocols. I had to be the "calm within the storm." I am now the one trained to have the presence of mind to yell the command "Call 911" and secure the scene until help arrives. All of this training and experience "should" have my instinct and/or knee jerk response now be one of calm, but instead I experience the opposite when I am with loved ones, especially children.

So why am I writing about this today? Last summer, my family and I witnessed a hit-and-run accident involving a pedestrian in front of my daughter's home. This is the home of my two precious grandsons, the loves of my life. For six months prior I had been wrestling with worst-case scenarios regarding the location of my daughter and her husband's beautiful house. Though a residential area, the tendency of the traffic which runs in front of their house is one of speed and disregard. I had an intense uneasiness regarding the safety of my grandchildren. I am embarrassed to admit that I had both day-dreamed and night-dreamed of horrific scenes. This is how my wounded mind works. So, to counteract those thoughts I had been sending up prayers of gratitude, love and protection. This usually keeps me from going a tad crazy from my possible obsessive thoughts.

On that summer evening, the street was busy with traffic, pedestrians and excitement as we all waited for the local fireworks to start. Then before my very eyes what I had been seeing in my mind's eye happened, but not to my grandchildren. The worst sound I have ever heard echoed across the lawn. Then the screams began.

My knee jerk: "OH MY GOD! SOMEONE JUST GOT HIT BY A CAR! CALL 911! CALL 911!" I heard my husband echo my call for help. I hysterically continued, "OH DEAR GOD, PLEASE NO, OHHHH NO NO NO, THEY HIT A KID. CALL 911, CALL 911. DEAR GOD, PLEASE HELP! NO NO NO!" as I turned and ran the other way.

Within a split second, something from deep within me, from another source that does not know fear, stopped me. It turned me around and had me step out of that old long-held fear. My hands instantly went up in motion and the healing frequencies started. I was drawn as if by a magnet to walk back and cross the street to the scene. My son-in-law was already there. I then saw that it was a woman who had been hit, not the young child I had seen standing on the sidewalk just before it all happened. The magnet of love pulled me in. I began to coo the scene into calm. First, I approached the young child who was crying in terror of what she had just witnessed. My hand instinctively hovered over her heart for a second as I looked her in the eye and said, "You are okay, love, you are okay, she is okay, love." Then, I looked at the lady who was trying to help the injured woman, who we learned was her aunt. Again, I made eye contact, my hand went up, I said the words, "You are okay, love, she is okay, love."

Together we held the injured woman. "It's okay, love, it's okay" was said a million times, all the while one of my arms and hand was moving and interacting with the healing frequencies while the other was helping, holding, embracing.

We positioned the injured lady on the grass, as comfortably as possible. The other woman eventually sensed a need to go tend to her daughter, the young girl who witnessed the accident. She told her aunt that she loved her, stood up and moved away. For what felt like an eternity, I sat holding the injured lady.

The police showed up and began assessing and questioning. I continued interacting with the healing frequencies and cooing, "It's okay, love, help is here, it's okay. It's okay, close your eyes and rest peacefully now. It's okay, love." My hand and arm continued to play, interact and receive the frequencies. By now my husband had taken a knee next to me, holding me as I held her. The container of love and peace which surrounded the scene was palpable. No one questioned what I was doing, there was no need. If they would have asked, I would not have had words. In that moment I had become an instrument of peace.

The ambulance arrived, I softly touched her head, said a gentle prayer and my goodbyes. My husband, son-in-law and I returned to the serenity of my grandchildren's home. "It's okay, love, it's okay" still vibrated through my body. "It's okay, love, it's okay."

We did not know what happened after we stepped away from the scene. We did not know the status of the injured lady. Nor did we know who or why someone would flee the scene after hitting someone. We just knew to continue to send and share love with ALL involved. That includes my grandchildren who witnessed extreme sights and sounds that night, and my daughter and son-in-law who need to continue to create a sanctuary of peace and safety in their home.

I do now know that my knee jerk, my innate instinctual response, is an instrument of peace. How is this so, how have I rewired my emotional encoding? I am not sure of the answer, but my gut, my head and my heart know that it may be because I have chosen to perceive this world, this universe, this dimension and my experiences with the eyes of Gratitude and Love. I have chosen Love over Fear. The battle was just an illusion, only LOVE resides here.

Just one week prior to that incident, I was strongly told by my inner guidance system to start using the Twin Hearts meditation on a daily basis. Obediently so, I had returned to my daily practice of this beautiful meditation based on the prayer of St. Francis. That prayer begins with "Make me an instrument of peace." That same week my daughter, listening to her internal guidance system, created a "You are Loved" affirmation art piece (a small wood round with those words painted on it) with a love note to go with it. Her intention: to share love.

The words of her LOVE NOTE include: "Place this affirmation in a place where you will see it daily. Say it out loud and feel the power of this statement. One day you will look at this affirmation and KNOW it to be true, you will feel the truth of these words run through your very being, lifting you to a new level of LOVE. On that day it is time to pass it forward. It is time for you to share the LOVE. Please gift this 'You are Loved' art along with this note to anyone you feel moved to share it with. It could be your best friend, a family member or better yet a stranger. The choice is always yours!"

A few moments prior to the accident, my daughter told me that she felt strongly compelled to place the affirmation art and note on the corner across the street. She told me she just wanted to leave it there for someone to find. And now we know why. I remain in deep gratitude for divine intervention. The whispers of our Creator reminding us that in every moment "It's okay, love, it's okay."

Dear lady, who was injured, and your family, the affirmation and note were intended for you! Dear person driving the vehicle, this note was also intended for you. We are ALL created in divine LOVE. Never forget, no matter what, always: You Are LOVED!

VIRGINIA "GINGER" ADAMS – Master Energy Healer, Intuitive Guide, Author, Artist and Creator of the Universal Gravity Code Program.

Virginia is a well-known motivator and medical practice administrator for over 28 years. Her dedication, integrity, and intuitive nature have positively impacted many healthcare practices and individuals around the world.

Years ago, Virginia received what she feels was a divine mandate to "Heal the Healer". Until that moment, she had described herself as a practical and methodical administrator. The seed planted by that mandate sent her on a path of discovery, ultimately leading to the opening of her Reconnective Healing® healthcare practice.

"Today I stand in immense gratitude for where my life path has guided me. Allow me to participate in your transformation from a fear-based life to one grounded in LOVE. You are LOVE! Tap into your inner wisdom and discover that you are your own expert. I remain honored and blessed" - Virginia Adams

Connect with Virginia
Virginia-Adams.com
gingersreconnection@gmail.com
+1 847 445 0092

Artwork by Christina Hladnik

I am grateful for ...

Week 10

Gratitude is riches. Complaint is poverty.

~ Doris Day

STAYING AFLOAT

There was a time, not too long ago, when gratitude was getting a lot of attention. It seemed everyone was talking about the importance of being grateful and the positive impact it had on their lives. Many self-help books recommended that individuals start gratitude journals to record the good things that happened in their lives. Intrigued, I bought a journal but found that after a long tiring day I lacked the energy and inspiration to write in it. Instead, I decided to start adding five things I was grateful for to my morning and evening prayers each day. This was easy at first, but as time went on it felt quite forced; I was just repeating the same things over and over. I knew that I was truly grateful, but somehow the gesture felt empty.

Then, one evening, I sat down to watch television and was immediately struck by how some of the people on the show had had a really tragic start in life. Some endured abuse or neglect; others, poverty or disease, and all of their stories really touched my heart. I realized in that moment that while my life was certainly not perfect, I had it better than a lot of people. As embarrassing as it is to admit, it sometimes takes another's tragedy to see our own good fortune.

That television series changed me forever; it changed how I viewed everything. The word gratitude took on a new meaning for me because I was finally able to feel it, truly feel it, resonating with my heart. Situations I once perceived as problematic now seemed insignificant and had no real significance in my life.

I also had so much more to include in my gratitude list each morning and night. Now, naming the five things to be grateful for came easily and from a different place within me. I felt as if my heart and eyes had opened, and everything that was good in my life, big or small, deserved to be recognized and celebrated.

As the parent of an adult child with special needs, my many happy experiences can be easily offset by the challenges. Difficult periods can last anywhere from minutes and hours to days, weeks, months and even years, and it is easy during these times to lose hope and let fear take over. The battle between the head and heart is fierce. One part of me wants to concentrate on my love for my son and my faith in God and His promises. The other part is tempted to believe that this will never end and is just how things are going to be for the rest of my life. This emotional tug-of-war is worse than any actual problem I'm facing, and gratitude has been the only antidote.

Though I've come a long way, that war is ongoing. To this day, a difficult situation concerning my son still catches me off-guard, like a sucker punch to the gut. What is different now is that I do not stay discouraged for long. Each time, the battle is a little shorter, and though I still get knocked to the ground, I do not stay down for long. No matter how I feel, I choose to move forward.

During times of struggle, I fight to quiet the voices in my head. I remind myself what my heart knows to be true and focus on everything I have to be grateful for in my life. I remember each time I have gotten through other difficult situations. Every time I recall a blessing it pulls me from the muck in my mind and brings me one step closer to finding peace while on this journey. It is not easy when your situation feels like the Titanic, but gratitude has become my floatation device.

We all know that life is made up of both good and bad times. There is no avoiding it. Sure, it is easy to be grateful when life is going our way; however, when in a season of struggle, it can feel like a thankless, full-time job. What I have learned is that gratitude is truly a light in the dark times. It is precisely when you are facing the largest challenges that you must remember why you are grateful. It may seem forced or untrue but chose to do it anyway. Allow yourself to fill up with thoughts that are light and positive. You will be surprised at where it leads you.

If you keep chasing, choosing and practicing it, gratitude will stay with you. It will become your first line of defense in difficult moments. When nothing external can bring you peace or joy, let gratefulness create a peaceful, internal oasis in which to rest until the storm passes. And it will.

LORI DECRESCENZO is a wife, mother and part-time Event Planner for a local non-profit organization. She enjoys crafting and reading, as well as writing; however, Lori is most passionate about stepping outside her comfort zone in an effort to continuously expand mentally and spiritually, and to help others do the same.

Connect with Lori
ldecrescenzo1@gmail.com

I am grateful for ...

Week 11

Gratitude makes sense of our past, brings peace for today, and creates a vision for tomorrow.

~ Melody Beattie

FINDING THE GRATITUDE IN THE MOST DIFFICULT SITUATIONS

We all have various life experiences, some are difficult and painful. Suffering a great loss can be difficult energy to move through. Loss comes in many forms; divorce, loss of any relationship, loss of a job, loss of health (presence of disease), and the loss of a loved one.

As we move through these experiences, it is important to feel and acknowledge the pain. Move through the journey of grief and honor the process. Loss can bring us into lower vibrational feelings such as, anger, guilt, and shame. As those feelings come up, I like to acknowledge them. Then as I move through them, I start talking to my inner child/self as if it were my own child. I tell myself all the loving things I would say to my own child that may be experiencing these feelings. When I am feeling guilty, I say, "everyone has their own journey, and you are not responsible for their journey and you cannot control anyone else or their actions." When I am feeling angry, I say, "Feel the anger, but then look for forgiveness and don't take it personal. It's usually about the other person, it's not about you." If I am feeling shame, I say, "it doesn't matter what other people think, their judgements are a reflection of them, not you."

It's okay to feel those feelings, but it is important to move the energy around them. This is the start of the healing process and is necessary to move your vibration to a higher state of peace, love, and happiness. In my own journey I found that the longer I stayed in the lower vibration, the more difficult it was to move into a higher vibrational place of peace and love.

We really operate in two modes, either love or fear. Often loss can bring about feelings of fear. I work hard to replace those feelings of fear with those of love. Having trust that there is a Devine purpose in everything that happens in our lives, trusting that everything is going to be okay, and trusting that these things are happening for you not to you provides a huge shift in energy. The most difficult situations can be our greatest teachers. These situations are all lessons to learn to help up grow and learn so we are ready for to move up to the next phase in our life.

In 2012, my boyfriend committed suicide. It was certainly one of the most difficult things I have ever had to go through. The real reality was, telling his three beautiful boys that their father was gone was the most difficult and each day it seemed even more difficult. That night, and the time to follow was an extreme journey of emotional pain for us all. I was angry, heart-broken, confused, and I missed him more every day. The questions of, why and all the what ifs were swarming my mind constantly. It was difficult to move through life in any kind of "normal" way. Getting back in life's routines, going to work every day and learning to start a new life without him proved to be very challenging. All I wanted was to get back to normal, but the truth was, it would never be the same. I had to learn to live life differently, without him.

His death was a huge wake up call for me. It was my rock bottom moment in my life. You see, I had a life of crazy relationships, full of addicts and alcoholics. I had been married twice and divorced, I had started over countless times. After I lost my boyfriend in such a traumatic way, I knew something needed to change. At the time, I did not know what or how, but I just knew I could not continue living the same anymore. I started the process of my own healing. I never realized how much I wasn't loving myself, setting boundaries and just simply putting myself first. I came to the realization that I wanted to feel needed and to have someone to take care of. As I walked my own healing journey, everything started to shift in my life and I mean EVERYTHING.

I will never forget the moment that I was waking in the morning, laying in my bed, my eyes were just opening, and I heard the birds singing their beautiful sound outside. I had lived in that house for years and not once had I ever noticed the birds. That day was like a movie in slow motion. As I got ready to leave the house, I noticed that I had the most amazing heighten sense of awareness. I walked out of the house and felt the sun hit me, I saw the butterflies landing on all the beautiful flowers around me. As I drove to work, I noticed every car and acknowledged every person with a smile. As I walked the parking lot to enter work, I noticed all the conversations around me and the overwhelming feeling I had to be grateful to be alive. I was now, for the first time in my life, present in the moment. I wasn't worrying about the past or the future, my brain wasn't swarming with all the things I had to do, there were no thoughts of anything other than the beauty of everything around me.

As a result of this tragic event in my life, I learned to love my self unconditionally, to set appropriate boundaries, to be present in each moment. I learned to have gratitude for everything from; waking up in the morning, being present, hearing the birds, noticing the flowers, acknowledging the people around me, my journey of healing and so much more.

The true healing took place once I moved out of the anger and moved into the energy of gratitude for the lessons that his death brought me. I look for the gifts in the most difficult situations, they are always there. We may not be able to see them right away, however, I promise you if you look you will find them. Find the gifts in the most difficult times and have gratitude for the lessons.

I now have a life filled with joy, happiness, and abundance all around me and I will not settle for anything less. For this journey, I give thanks for the great lessons and the opportunity to grow.

KIM RICHARDSON is a personal chef, health coach, best-selling author, and publisher, teaching others how to live in a High Vibrational place of peace, love, and joy. Kim has a real love and passion for food, cooking and teaching how food plays a role in the mind, body, spirit connection.

Through sharing her own personal experiences, she empowers individuals to transform their lives. She helps individuals to heal, forgive and expand without judgment. Her passion is helping people discover their true gifts and how to use them in the world. Kim teaches with unconditional love as she hopes it will have a ripple effect in the world.

Kim resides in Northern Arizona where she enjoys the warm weather and sunshine with her husband, Symon and their fur baby, Hudson. To learn more about Kim's work and download your free recipe, visit her website.

Connect with Kim
Kimrichardson.kim
Facebook @kimrichardson444
YouTube @ goo.gl/8Q5RiW

I am grateful for ...

Week 12

In ordinary life, we hardly realize that we receive a great deal more than we give, and that it is only with gratitude that life becomes rich.

~ Dietrich Bonhoeffer

A STEPMOTHER'S GIFT OF UNCONDITIONAL LOVE

Gifts of healing come from the most unexpected places. I am sharing my story of gratitude in hope that others can see the gift that is being offered in the most difficult situations. My father expressed many regrets about his relationship with my sister and I during the last year of his life. Due to a long history battling the disease of alcohol, my father was often physically and emotionally abusive to my sister and I. I believe that my father also struggled with untreated mental health since the toxic behaviors that my father exhibited in his relationships continued during his 30 years of sobriety. My father's physical abuse of my sister ultimately resulted in the dissolution of my parent's marriage after 17 years. Since high school graduation, my father spent many years absent from my life including the lives of my children due to his disease, missing many important milestones, which caused significant suffering in our lives and feelings of not being good enough. Since if a father could abandon you, I internalized that I was not loveable, and love is betrayal.

The energy of feeling not good enough and not loving myself permeated through my life. I can now see the energy patterns throughout my life where people I loved ended in betrayal. Although my father was absent from my life, I worked my way through college by working multiple jobs, married, had two beautiful healthy children and built a thriving business as an electrical engineer.

When my kids were young, my husband was killed by a drunk driver and cancer took my mom away too young. Most would look at my life and think I had a great life, but the lack of self-love blocked all lasting internal joy from my life. Later, after years and years of suffering, I started my spiritual journey to return to my truth and loving myself.

During my spiritual journey, I eventually came to believe that my father did the best he could and showed up perfectly in my life for my soul's expansion. During the last year of my father's life, I was able to have insight and forgiveness for my father's life journey especially in areas that mirrored my life including feelings of not being loved and love is betrayal. In this short story of gratitude, I want to share how the beautiful soul of my stepmother showed up in this lifetime to create a catalyst for allowing both my father and I to feel unconditional love in the last few weeks of his life.

After my parents' divorce, my father went on to marry three women. After a few years my father ended each marriage by emotionally abandoning each woman. I feel that this is because my father took on a belief like I did as a child that love was betrayal. My father's way to handle emotion was to run away before he was betrayed so he would quickly end relationships and run away to fish. In Louisiana, he left one wife while she was at work and moved to Florida. My sister was left to support her emotionally. I can now look back and see that my sister and I were both left to emotionally support each of his wives. The emotional dissolution of each of his marriages was only a reminder of the pain that we experienced when he abandoned us in high school. The last few years of his life, my father married his last wife a second time. She is the stepmother who ultimately unknowingly provided my father and I with a beautiful priceless gift of healing a lifetime of trauma that allowed us both to feel unconditional love.

Everyone knows that I love doing "talk-text" and when I was texting my stepmother the software would translate her name to Buddy. She was indeed my Buddy in this lifetime. The last time my father abandoned me was when my mother died. I called with an emotional request that he meet me at the hospital. He agreed but never came. I was devastated again. After years of suffering, I realized that he did not show up at the hospital because he didn't love me, but because he loved my mother and I deeply. He could not handle the emotion around her death, so he ran away.

My children and I reconnected with my father the last year of his life including regular visits to Texas, letters and calls. My children were a tremendous source of joy to my dad and he said so often. I even drove from my California home to stay with him in Texas for the last two weeks of his life while he was in Rehab. During my time with my father, he shocked me when he indicated that he wanted to make up for his past transgressions by providing some inheritance in his will for me. I was always financially secure and often helped other family members financially. I was touched by my father's wish since he was a miser with money growing up. I remember when my sister and I were going to girl scout camp and my mother wanted to buy us a new night gown, however she cried when my father refused and indicated that she should give us her old night gowns. My father leaving me any type of inheritance was not about money, but the thought made me somehow feel that my father loved me.

My Buddy was angry that my father wanted to leave me an inheritance and threatened to leave him. Three months before my father died, I witnessed a fight where my Buddy was in a rage over my father wanting to leave me an inheritance. Ironically, I was staying out of the fight by staring down at a book on the table that she gave me that morning called Know Your Worth. My Buddy had asked me if I wanted the book from a box she obtained from a garage sale. My children returned with me for another visit a few weeks later prior to me spending the last two weeks of my father's life with him.

Although my father preferred to be home with his wife and beloved dog, Crockett, he enjoyed his two weeks with the staff and I at the rehab center after his extended hospital stay. During the two weeks, my heart was full seeing my young, 77-year-old father busy all day with a twinkle in his eye! I loved seeing him get stronger each day and even hopeful for the future. When I returned to sleep at night, my Buddy would say things like your father doesn't want you here or, don't encourage your father to come home since he was approved for 100 days. Also, my Buddy created a multitude of situations including lying to my father trying to have him request that I leave to sabotage my inheritance. However, my Buddy was a catalyst for the opposite, my father and I ended up having the most authentic conversations that we've never had in this lifetime.

I am so grateful for those difficult emotionally charged conversations that my Buddy drove my father and I to have while both completely vulnerable. We were able to express ourselves with a strong knowing that the other person would still love us. I had a habit of recording most of my father's conversations, so I am blessed that they help me remember the love that I didn't feel all my life. During our discussions, I was also able to see generational energy patterns of lack of self-love, inheritance and feeling trapped in relationships. I am in the process of writing an entire book on those big AHA moments, including the ones with my father that we came jointly into this life time to clear.

I discovered if I allowed myself to become the observer of my own life energy patterns including how generational inheritance energy showed up that it was easier to transmute the energy for my life and future generations. Most would see my Buddy's actions during the last few months of my father's life as undesirable and both my father and I didn't deserve that kind of treatment. However, I see the priceless gift that she provided to my father and I, we were both able to be vulnerable and speak authentically, especially in the last two weeks of his life. My father transitioned from his physical body in this lifetime knowing that he is safe to be vulnerable. He also now knows that love does not have to be a betrayal. I am so grateful that I was able to "feel" unconditional love and gain a "knowing" that I am enough. My buddy's gift to "know my worth" helped clear an inheritance energy thread flowing through our family.

Dad, I am so grateful that I was able to hold your hand when you took your last breath and share the last two weeks of your life remembering the love and wonderful memories that can now replace all the suffering from the years, we were apart. Thanks to your wife, my Buddy; You and I know we are loved unconditionally.

PAULA OBEID shares her love with the world as Chief Creative Officer at Bliss Always and Pure at Home. As a Master Hypnotherapist and NATH Transpersonal Hypnotherapy Trainer, Reiki Master, Aromatherapist, Intuitive Life & Business coach, she can help individuals achieve personal or business goals through a mind, body and soul approach.

Paula is a holistic instructor and author who assists others using her intuition, training on various modalities and knowledge gained from her life experiences. Utilizing intuitive reflective listening skills, she motivates individuals that are ready to create change in their life.

Paula works with clients to reach their full potential and goals utilizing proven effective strategies and modalities. Paula facilitates clients obtaining insight into their life purpose and achieving their dreams. Her passions are reflected in her heart-centered endeavors that provide services, education and products that allow individuals to lovingly move through life with joy and ease.

Connect with Paula
Blissalways.com
pureathome.com

I am grateful for ...

Week 13

Imagine you have a bright light within you.
When you look at something with gratitude and
feel appreciation, it is as if the bright light within you
is shining beams of love and light out. Some of it
may touch what you are looking at and some
of it falls on the surroundings.

~ Your Angels

GRATITUDE PUTS THE SPRING BACK IN MY STEP

Gratitude has helped me in different ways, throughout my life. The best way I can explain this is to think of gratitude as a helper. In telling you my story, I am hoping it will inspire you to have gratitude in your toolbox when things in your life are getting difficult and you are unsure where to turn for help.

I spent more than half of my life in the corporate world. I went with a friend to apply because that is what the expectation seemed to me. I did get hired and for so many of the years I was there I absolutely loved my job. I had several wonderful managers throughout my corporate life, who truly cared and mentored me on my journey.

There was a time though, that was not quite as happy for me and the manager I had was not quite what I would refer to as mentor material. There were many changes which we had not experienced before in the company. It was the first time ever when people were being let go, departments were there one day and gone the next, new divisions being formed, others being merged and on it went.

The department I was in was misunderstood as it was a newer function to the company. I was the manager of between 20 - 35 people. I had recently had to let some of them go. It was not an easy time for my team.

During all of these transitions, I realized one day, as I was walking to my office from the parking ramp, that I had no more spring in my step. People would comment I walked with a spring and on this particular day, it was gone. It didn't happen in just one day, this just happened to be the day I noticed it.

The smile that was generally found on my face and the typical happy me, had somehow left the building without me being aware of the change.

I did not want this to be who I was. I enjoyed having a springy step. I loved smiling at everyone as I walked down the halls to meetings to bring a little more brightness into their day. I wanted to feel the joy of being there again, the gratitude for all the wonderful things that surrounded me each day.

I knew I had to do something different than I was doing. I decided right in that moment, I would take a few minutes after each meeting (I was in meetings 75% of my day at least), to list what I was grateful for, about the meeting that just happened.

This may sound like a strange thing to do, not the gratitude part but the gratitude for the meeting I just came out of. It made the most sense to me because there were so many things as a whole, I was still feeling grateful for, but the meetings and the under current was a different story. I knew, deep within, to get back to the happy me with the spring in my step, I needed to find gratitude in everything, the good and the not so good.

After each meeting, I would list three things that happened out of the meeting that were positive and that I was grateful for. Even during the meetings at times, I was mentally creating my list. The shift within me started rather quickly because now I was searching for gratitude instead of letting the energy of the meetings consume me.

I will admit some meetings I really had to search for the gratitude. It was the coffee I was drinking some meetings, or that I was able to see the sun shining outside during the meeting. Other meetings I could literally feel the gratitude flowing through me from the Angels who I would ask to join me. The Angels would clear the energies of the room and fill it with love and gratitude. There were some meetings I would walk out smiling. Thank you, Angels.

I realized I had the spring back in my step within just a day or so, once I set my mind to looking for the gratitude with each meeting. I had a smile on my face walking into my office each morning. I was grateful to be there, and I continued to find things throughout my day and through all of the meetings, to be grateful for.

The Angels were there with me every step of the way cheering me on and assisting me on the gratitude path of getting my spring and smile back in my life.

We all have different times in our lives when life seems to be running us. Finding the gratitude amongst even some of the most challenging times may be what can help you with the spring in your step and the smile on your face.

Angel Blessings to you.

SUE BROOME is a gifted intuitive healer and spiritual teacher. She works with the Divine and Angels in guiding others on their spiritual healing journey. She shares tools of empowerment in each session and is available for healings and readings which offer guidance from the Angels.

Sue is a host with International Angels Network. Angel Talk with Sue is available Wednesdays at 9pm ET. This allows her to reach a global audience.

She loves sharing with others how to connect with their Loved Ones through her book, Signs from Your Loved Ones and her courses. Memories shared with your Loved Ones is currently available as a free course.

Sue works with groups, individuals in private healing sessions and continues to create online courses and products. Sessions are available through phone, email or Skype.

Enjoy Healing Tools from the Angels, a gift, a PDF to work with the Angels: empowerment4you.com/angel-talk-with-sue

Connect with Sue:
Empowerment4You.com
su.broome@gmail.com
Instagram @SueBroome44
YouTube @ bit.ly/SueBroomeYouTube
Radio show @ InternationalAngelsNetwork.com/Sue

I am grateful for ...

Week 14

Enjoy the little things, for one day you may look back and realize they were big things.

~ Robert Brault

A LITTLE RED BIKE

The Lesson Today

"Three plus one equals...?" Ms. Ratcliffe asked.

"I've got a new bike!" I blurted out with all the exuberance of a six-year-old, "I've got a new bike!"

It was all I could talk about in class that day. In fact, I probably hijacked the lesson in the way a child with special educational needs can sometimes do. Did this amazing teacher show any sign of exasperation? No, she didn't. Instead, she seemed so interested in my bike, I asked if she would come and see it.

"I'd love to," she replied, "Let's see it at home-time!"

No Average Child

As I swaggered out into the playground with Ms. Ratcliffe by my side, I felt as proud as could be. We met my mother at the school gate and together the three of us walked to the bike shed where my shiny red bike was standing like a loyal steed. I was so excited to show my teacher my new love and demonstrate my newly acquired skill - riding! I remember Ms. Ratcliffe clapping and then waving me goodbye as I unsteadily peddled off with my mum striding by my side.

No Average Teacher

Ms. Ratcliffe! I can still recall her name nearly half a century later. Her kindness left a lasting impression on me. It was the sort of kindness that came from a patient soul who knew that there was more to life than academic achievement.

Perhaps she stood out to me because there were other teachers who were not so kind. Back then people did not appreciate dyslexia and other learning challenges as they do today. In addition to not being able to comprehend much of what was taught, I had a speech impediment and was not easy to understand. Some teachers decided shouting loudly was the best way to help me absorb the lessons. It didn't work. I don't remember Ms. Ratcliffe ever shouting, only smiling.

Years later, I would return to that school to be interviewed to join the teaching staff. I was disappointed when I asked after Ms. Ratcliffe and no one remembered her. I would have liked to thank her for all she had given me. But when I thought about it, I realized I was able to thank her, because I was given a chance to pass her kindness and compassion along to other children.

Defying Odds

My primary school headmaster told my mother that I would not get any formal qualifications and she needed to rethink my future. But I did get them; in fact, I exceeded all expectations. I achieved a master's in education, specializing in children under five, became a teacher and then an Assistant Head. I set an intention to be the type of teacher I remember Ms. Ratcliffe being. I wanted to be more than a sharer of knowledge, the marker of work and the controller of behavior. I wanted to be a catalyst for change and to make a difference in people's lives.

When we teach, there is something far greater than just the subject matter involved. True teaching is about igniting in a child something that remains long after the lesson has ended; it is about facilitating a shift in perspective, a resilience for learning, a determination to succeed and a sense of feeling valued. A child's potential cannot always be determined by who they are today. We can never be sure what factors will inspire or hold them back, support or compromise them; we cannot know whether they will see the sunshine or the clouds in life. What we can do is try our best to give them strategies that help them to learn, to feel worthy and to feel valued as individuals.

Academic attainment is a goal of education, but it is not the only one. There are powerful intangible benefits for individuals and for society when teachers make a difference at a soul level. Ms. Ratcliffe is proof of that.

Gratitude

I am grateful for so much. Sometimes I can see the blessing in the moment and give thanks where it is due. Other times, the appreciation occurs days, months, or even years later.

There are many ways to live in gratitude and there are many ways to express that gratitude. Never underestimate the value of being able to pass gratitude along to others. By so doing you expand the positive energy in ever-increasing circles, impacting lives in more ways than you can imagine.

Living in gratitude includes:

- ♥ Appreciating when you can offer thanks to someone today.
- ♥ Appreciating the ways you can offer thanks by passing it forward.

Each day, say a positive affirmation such as, I am constantly surrounded by reasons to be grateful. This will keep your vibration high and your focus on appreciating the good in your life.

TONIA BROWNE is a bestselling author, teacher and coach. She is a strong advocate of inviting fun into our lives and encouraging people to see their world from a new perspective. Tonia's writing includes coaching strategies interspersed with spiritual insights and personal anecdotes.

She takes a holistic approach to change and believes in liberating the inner child within us. As a teacher, Tonia has worked in the United Kingdom and internationally for over twenty years and was an Assistant Head for seven.

She is a Heal Your Life® Workshop Leader, Coach and Business Trainer. Tonia's book Spiritual Seas: Diving into Life: 12 Strategies for Riding the Waves of Life reached Amazon Number 1 Ranking in both the USA and the UK. Dive into her new book Mermaids: An Empath and Introvert's Guide to Riding the Waves of Life, Diving into Life Series.

Connect with Tonia
toniabrowne.com

I am grateful for ...

Week 15

*If God said, "Rumi, pay homage to everything
that has helped you enter my arms.," there would
not be one experience of my life, not one thought,
not one feeling, not any act I would not bow to.*

~ Rumi

THE GRATEFUL "GOOSE"

When asked to count our blessings, it becomes very easy to gravitate towards the people, places or events that warm our hearts; the smile of a loving grandmother, a financial windfall, or the affection of a loyal pet. But as Rumi points out in the previous quote, what is more challenging is to recall the times that brought us much emotional or physical pain and offer gratitude for THOSE challenges that present themselves in our lives. Some cancer survivors refer to this dreaded disease as the greatest blessing in their lives. While I've never had to experience the consequences of living with cancer, I did have to deal with a lifelong struggle that is common to many people today.

Ever since I can remember I was always a chubby kid. Brought up in an Italian-American home, food was always a focal point of our family. Sunday dinners, holidays and family gatherings always involved aunts, uncles, cousins and family friends sitting around a table of incredibly home cooked meals meticulously and lovingly prepared by my mother and grandmother. Because of the joy and laughter related to these events, food for me became a substitute for love. It became my emotional uplift in times of despair. But my body didn't take too kindly to this type of eating and it was always a constant struggle to keep my weight down. As a result, growing up, I was always one of the heaviest kids in my school. This led to some not so fond events.

My earliest memories of gym class in grade school stand-out because they were fraught with emotional upheaval. While everyone was having fun playing "Duck, Duck Goose", I hated it. You can guess who everyone picked to be the "Goose"." Let me tag Anthony, he won't catch me." I logged more miles running circles around classmates than all the Shuttle missions took around the earth combined. During one gym class we had to perform basic calisthenics and there was a row of us lying on our backs, knees up, waiting for the whistle to blow to see how many sit-ups we could perform in 5 minutes. We had a friend holding our ankles and counting the reps. Paul was my friend holding my ankles. When the gym teacher blew the whistle, all the kids were bouncing up and down easily and effortlessly, and there I was, struggling to do ONE. The frustration and embarrassment grew more intense as time was marching on and I couldn't get my elbows to my knees just... one... time. Luckily, the principal came in to talk to our gym teacher who then became distracted and was no longer watching us. When time was up and he went down the row asking the counters how many sit-ups we all performed, all I could hear as I was lying on my back, staring at the ceiling, were absurd numbers: 143, 174, 215!

The embarrassment and apprehension swelled within me as I could feel my heart pounding when he got to Paul. However, Paul astutely knew the teacher wasn't paying attention, so rather than embarrass me, he told him I did 70! I was speechless. The tension left my body like air out of a balloon. I dodged another fat embarrassment moment. For countless years following, I tried many attempts to solve this problem with diet books, pills and exercise machines but nothing worked.

After I got accepted into Chiropractic school, the intensity to solve this problem accelerated. I was determined to graduate a thin and healthy doctor. My focus turned to more popular, commercial programs. But as soon as I stopped doing these programs, my weight FLEW back on and brought with it friends. I felt like I was spending my whole life trying to keep a beach ball underwater, and if I let go, that proverbial beach ball of fat would fly sky high into Weight Watchers heaven. Within the next few years I gained over 140 pounds as my weight ballooned up to 340 pounds. Frustration was soon replaced with hopelessness and despair. I was left with the realization that I would remain very heavy, unhealthy and living with the physical and emotional consequences for the rest of my life, however short that may be. But as I once read in a spiritual journal, God hides in the bushes, meaning the events in our life that appear to be the most meaningless can be the most life altering.

One weekend, while visiting my parents, my brother (who was struggling with weight issues of his own), placed an ad for a doctor supervised weight loss program on an end table that I accidentally stumbled upon. Something inside me told me to give it a try, so I did.

On October 5th, 2014, I checked in at the NurtiMost office in Boardman, Ohio with a 320-pound attitude of "I don't know if this will work, but what the hell, let's give it a try". By December 9th ,2015, I was 205 pounds of "I can't believe I'm at this weight!" The program literally changed my physiology and relationship with food and the horrible addictions to sweets I had my entire life. The binge eating Hostess Cupcake days were gone and replaced with sneaking kale chips into movie theaters...and loving every bit of it.

Because of the success I had on the program and my background as a chiropractor, I was offered an opportunity by Dr. James Leone to counsel patients on the NutriMost program. I now incorporate this into my practice.

However, had I not had the lifetime struggle with food and sugar addiction, I would have been an outsider looking in. Like sitting in a movie theater, watching and enjoying a movie but ready to leave after the credits start rolling. But this is different. I'm IN the movie. I AM one of the characters. When someone walks into our office and begins to tell me their struggles, I AM them. There is nothing that anyone has ever told me that I can't relate to; the despair, frustration and hopelessness of trying every conceivable option out there, only to see a problem get worse. The fear of more serious health challenges awaiting while feeling that my days are now being numbered. Been there, ate that.

I am now grateful for this enduring challenge. As a result, my perspective on gratitude has expanded to also be thankful for the struggles that are inevitably encountered in our lives. Blessing these setbacks has allowed God's grace to permeate my soul. And when this happens, negative emotions such as fear, depression and anger have no room to percolate. Perhaps the great Master teacher Jesus alluded to this by saying: "The mind can't serve two masters: for either he will hate the one and love the other; or else he will hold to the one and despise the other" (Mathew 6:24). Interpreting this through a metaphysical prism, it is impossible to be in a mental state of gratitude and depression simultaneously. Therefore, the quickest way out of feeling the blues is to cultivate gratitude! But the beauty is we don't have to look "big picture" here.

Start with anything to be thankful for. Try this experiment that Derek Rydall, best¬-selling author of Emergence and The Abundance Project, writes in his books. Pick something as mundane as putting gas in your car. As your standing at the pump, instead of thinking of all the things on your "to do" list that need to get done, or the fight you just had with your boss or spouse, think of all the people that conspired to get that gasoline in your car: the driver of the tanker that delivered the gas to the gas station, the people that built that pump, those working in the refinery that "made" the gasoline as well as the workers in the well that pumped the oil from the oceans, etc. You get the idea.

There is SO much to be thankful for EVERY day, we just need to make the effort to look.

And when we do, our lives change because the spirit of gratitude is now emerging FROM us. We're not being dependent on people or external circumstances to determine how we feel. As we express gratitude daily, we open the way for the beautiful moments in life to repeat themselves and increase in magnitude because the universe will match our energy and bring us more events, people and circumstances to be thankful FOR.

As I counsel patients daily, I often reflect on my grade school years and am forever thankful for always being the "goose", hopelessly chasing classmates endlessly around a gym of laughing children. It has blessed me in ways I could never have imagined. And by the way, I recently connected with my grade school friend Paul on Facebook and thanked him for having my back all those years ago.

DR. ANTHONY BERARDINO is a 1992 graduate of Logan College of Chiropractic in Chesterfield, Missouri and has been practicing chiropractic for 26 years. He specializes in a functional neurology technique called Quantum Neurology and is also a certified Primal Restoration Specialist, focusing on ancestrally-based ketogenic nutrition.

His office is located in Strongsville, Ohio. Dr. Berardino is available for nutrition and weight loss counseling either in person, or by phone. To learn more about the NutriMost Wellness and Weight Loss Program visit: NutriMost.com and NutriMostReviews.com

Connect with Anthony
drberardino@outlook.com
440-268-9502

I am grateful for ...

_____
_____
_____
_____
_____
_____
_____
_____
_____
_____
_____
_____
_____
_____
_____
_____
_____
_____
_____
_____
_____
_____
_____
_____
_____
_____
_____
_____
_____
_____
_____
_____
_____
_____
_____
_____
_____

Week 16

Gratitude is a powerful catalyst for happiness.
It's the spark that lights a fire of joy in your soul.

~ Amy Collette

CONNECT WITH NATURE'S BEAUTY & ABUNDANCE

I believe nature is here to inspire us to live, dream and create, and to remind us who we really are. I see nature as our inspiration for everyday living. And, for that we must be grateful.

After a divorce and a challenging relationship, I spent a lot of solo time in nature rebuilding myself. The beach was my go-to spot, and I could often be found reading in a hammock hung between two elegant driftwood trees or just looking out over the beautiful aqua gulf waters. Being there gave me comfort, security and inspiration to live life more fully than I ever had before.

There was something magical about this beach, with its beautiful, white, fine sand and abundance of weathered driftwood. It faced west and was both hidden and easily visible at the same time. Above all, it exuded a powerful energy that attracted visitors – couples, families, little girls skipping like sea fairies, fishermen, teens, models and lovers - from all around the world. I noticed that people were drawn to touch and feel the energy of the trees, and one in particular, which I affectionately dubbed The Beauty Tree.

What, I wondered, was it about these trees that drew people in and energized them?

I began to look at the fine details to see what stories the tree had to tell and saw grains, markings and limb breakage that were not perfect and, at the same time, were beyond perfection. I watched how the sand changed over time to expose or hide different parts of the tree. The awe of this tree gave me the inspiration and reminder that we all need to connect with nature. In Gratitude. It leads to synchronicities in life that help you remember who you are, and in my belief, that is why we are here. Nature's beauty reminds us to connect with our physical world, connect with each other (because we are one) and be our very best, grounded selves.

Mother nature is Feminine with her abundant beauty.

We are one.

We all are beautiful in our own unique way.

Be inspired by nature. Be inspired by Nature's Beauty.

Nature also contains an abundance of possibilities. Possibilities is such a deep insightful word, and I love everything about it - how it rolls off your tongue, how its syllables bounce off each other, and even how it looks on paper. But what I most love is its meaning. Possibility is derived from the Latin word, possibilitās, meaning able to be done.

If we are here to remember who we are, part of that must be to support others to do the same - to dream, inspire and create.

Nature's beauty also teaches us of abundance at its purest level. I took a class based on John Randolph Price's book, The Abundance Book, a key concept of which is the lavish abundance of creation. In order to understand this concept more fully we talked about how many blades of grass there are, and how grass so easily grows and replenishes. Infinite abundance. I radiate infinite abundance at all times is a quote to repeat during the ten-step process to internalize and integrate this and other concepts. Most of all the book teaches us that a true understanding of abundance is founded upon gratitude, for it is gratitude for what we already have that keeps the flow of abundance and health for our Earth.

We need to be grateful for all of nature's beauty. Each and every day, at every moment. We are the same energy as nature. We are one. Therefore, we also need to be grateful for our individual beauty. Self-love stems from within. It gives us the power to create, dream, and be inspired. We know we are powerful creators, just as nature is. We know well the power of nature – we see it in the form of waves, tsunamis, hurricanes, tornadoes, as well as its power to grow, sustain, and provide. We also know the heart-warming power of flowers, dragonflies, dolphins, whales and ladybugs. It is all part of nature's infinite beauty.

Everything in nature is made up of patterns, structures, and designs, from the smallest atom to the infinite universe. Experts call these patterns sacred geometry; take the time to look and you will see them as well. These are nature's beloved artwork and the structure for everything. They are a reminder to us to celebrate, and be grateful for, everything in our lives, from the largest blessing to the smallest, seemingly mundane, everyday miracle.

LEANN SPOFFORD is an experienced Marketing Director, Brand Expert, and Nature Enthusiast. She is the Founder of Creative Content Connects. Leann helps businesses remember their "why" and creatively communicates that "why" so they connect with their customers and others.

Leann is known for her unique branding process: Remember Who You Are. She helps people, business and nature prosper together. Leann is committed to building businesses who advance healthy oceans, nurture nature human potential and human kindness. She created Nature's Beauty Project to raise the conscious awareness of our planet and the inspiration from nature's beauty.

Leann is currently writing Nature's Beauty Inspires – think Buddha and Louis Vuitton take a walk together in nature.

Connect with Leann
creativecontentconnects.com
Facebook @ leann.spofford
Nature's Beauty Facebook Page @ NaturesBeautyProject
LinkedIn @ linkedin.com/in/leann-spofford

I am grateful for ...

Week 17

The more grateful I am, the more
beauty I see.

~ Mary Davis

AN ATTITUDE OF GRATITUDE

Life was difficult. I had a job that I despised. Finances were tough. I felt like I was trapped. Nowhere to go. No options. No choices. I was at a breaking point. I curled up on the lawn chair and just cried. I felt like there was no way forward. I didn't know what to do.

It was 2008. I had been at my job for less than a year. My career as a mortgage professional abruptly ended in 2007 when the mortgage market crashed. I took this job because it was the first job that I was offered, and I needed to work.

Now, mind you, I was completely miserable in my mortgage career too. I wanted something more in my life. I wanted my work to be fulfilling. Mortgage wasn't doing it for me. So, when the market crashed, I decided that day that I would not return to a career in mortgage. I searched for months for a new career, all the while our savings was dwindling. If I didn't find work soon, we were going to lose the house.

I was ecstatic when I got the job offer. I remember sitting in my living room talking to the recruiter. I was so happy. I didn't care how low the pay was going to be or how boring it sounded because I needed the job. And then the recruiter told me what my salary would be. I was shocked. So shocked that I had to ask him to repeat the number to me. It was much higher than I expected. This was a gift. I was grateful. Although, I didn't realize what a gift until much, much later.

Now, let's get back to the lawn chair. I haven't mentioned that I was talking to my husband when I curled up on that chair balling my eyes out. I was telling him how I just couldn't do it any longer. I had to get out of that job and I didn't know what to do next. He sat there, carefully listening to what I was saying. When I started to calm down, he said something to me that changed my life forever. He said, "If you could do something different, what is it that you would do?" I was stunned. I had no idea what I wanted to do. No clue at all. I had my drawings - the Enchanted Elementals - but I had no idea what I was to do with them. How could I not know what I truly wanted?

After some contemplation, and reading quite a few self-improvement books, I knew that if my life were to change, I would be the only person who could create the change. No one could do it for me. The only option I had was to change my perception of the world I was in. It was going to require me to have faith when I didn't know what was next, to trust when I couldn't see the road ahead, and to do something so radical that it required me to step outside my comfort zone. I needed to appreciate what I already had. To understand that I'm always guided to the right place at the right time. To know that it was going to be okay. I recognized that in order to shift my circumstances and situation, I was going to need an Attitude of Gratitude. This wasn't easy. The journey of gratitude can be a rough one. Sometimes circumstances and situations suck. They feel like they are taking us down and we can't find our way back. Sometimes it can be difficult to find something to be grateful for.

Our greatest obstacle on the path to a life filled with gratitude is our thoughts and the key to the path of gratitude is our thoughts. Think about that for a moment. We are what we think we are. What we focus on multiplies. We create our circumstances and situations with our thoughts. How we respond to situations stems from our thoughts. Positivity comes from our thoughts. Negativity comes from our thoughts. Do you see the common denominator here? Our thoughts are what we need to pay attention to. If we are constantly saying that our job sucks and we keep looking for all the reasons why it sucks, then our job is going to suck. Period.

Now, what happens when we start looking for what's good in our job, our relationships, or whatever it is we want to improve? We find it. When I began to look at my job from a different perspective, I realized that the job was truly a gift. It was a bridge to my next endeavor, although I had no clue at the time what that would be. It supported my family. It gave me the opportunity to build and sharpen my skills for my future endeavor. It provided me with everything I needed. But these things didn't come to me immediately. It took time to shift my mindset and my thoughts. It took time to see what was good. And often times, I had to stretch myself to find the good in my job. What I found, was that I had to surrender. I had to stop resisting. I had to stop trying to find a way out and embrace what I already had.

Over the years I've experienced many trials and tribulations in my job. It's just been the last several years that I really understand what a gift my job has been and continues to be. Yes, I am still in that same job, 11 years later. And no, it's not exactly where I want to be, but it's taking time for me to create my next endeavor - it's a process that continues to grow and evolve too. This job is fully supportive of what I am creating. It is the bridge that is safely carrying me along the road that is less traveled.

All these years I have learned how to shift circumstances by practicing an Attitude of Gratitude. It's a lifelong practice. As we grow and evolve, our Attitude of Gratitude does too. I have applied this to every area of my life. It has transformed me in ways I never expected.

Now that you know some of my story, I'd like to share with you my process for having an Attitude of Gratitude. First, decide what it is you want to shift. Is it a career? A relationship? Your health? Finances? Next, begin to pay attention to your thoughts around this thing you want to change. What is it you say when you talk about it? What words do you find yourself using? What emotions are you generating around it? How do you perceive the situation or circumstance?

For instance, in my job, I felt like my manager was working against me. I was so frustrated with him and felt totally unsupported. And then, I realized that my attitude was the reason he wasn't supporting me. Although we had a good relationship, I was always frustrated with how he handled things. He didn't handle things the way I thought he should have, which translated into the fact that I didn't support him. Once I realized I was doing this, I slowly began to look for the good things about him. I began to accept him for who he was, not who I wanted him to be. And wouldn't you know, our relationship began to shift. Today, I feel completely supported in my work. I was able to shift the relationship because I became aware of the way I perceived him and decided to shift that perception to one of appreciation and gratitude.

Once you pay attention to your thoughts, you will start to see where the negativity creeps in, where you are triggered, what things you say, you think, and what you do. Remember that you can shift whatever it is by looking for the good in it. If you can't find something good, make something up.

Lastly, practice this every day. Like I said earlier, this is not a one-time deal. It is a lifetime practice. The goal is to go to bed every night and find at least one thing you are grateful for. If possible, write it down. If that doesn't work for you, tell yourself as you are drifting off to sleep. As you develop this practice of an Attitude of Gratitude, I promise you will start to see an amazing shift in your life.

Emylea, the Enchanted Elemental for Gratitude, is on the next page waiting for you to color her. You may want to journal with her, you'll be amazed with the insight that comes forth.

ROBIN CARLTON is an Artist, Intuitive, and Teacher who thrives on helping others find the tools and resources that encourage the exploration of imagination, color, intuition, and symbolism.

Robin is the owner and facilitator of Ladies Healing Day, an annual event in Phoenix, Arizona. She is also the founder and managing editor of ArizonaMindBodySpirit.com and the creator of the Enchanted Elementals, who are guides that help you to tap in to your inner guidance. She has also published two decks of empowerment cards.

If you'd like to download the full-size version of her coloring page, receive additional guidance for an Attitude of Gratitude, and other resources, and visit her website.

Connect with Robin
robincarlton.com/p/52weeks

Artwork by Robin Carlton

I am grateful for ...

Week 18

*We can only be said to be alive in those
moments when our hearts are conscious of or treasures.*

~ Thornton Wilder

FROM GRIEF TO GRATITUDE

One of the best gifts that we can share and receive as humans is gratitude. The best thing about gratitude is that it's free, and at its minimum, we are giving and receiving the maximum inspiration, appreciation, and kindness behind it.

This beautiful gift, this wondrous emotion, is an element that can heal broken patches in the heart. The simplicity of giving and being open to receive washes out the pain and hurt and replaces it with appreciation and generosity.

How do we learn to be open to gratitude? Embodying gratitude looks overwhelming, but it's a daily practice. Like growing a flower, we must start by planting a seed. This seed of gratitude must be planted with its best intention. Once we bury this seed, we nurture it with love, kindness, warm wishes, and we go on with our lives. As simple as this sounds, gratitude works the rest. We awake to a day of unknowingness, and we embrace its unknown quality of beauty, lessons, joy, laughter, and possible new memories. Once we become grateful for the day ahead, the seed grows its roots and expands into the soil. Practicing small, random acts of kindness is the sprout to gratitude. This is where we trust the process of change. At some point in your day, share a warm smile with a stranger, call a loved one to hear their voice, appreciate something of nature outdoors, give a hug — or two!

At this point, a small seed has grown its precious petals. It comes to full bloom when we begin to practice this mindless task. Sounds simple right? But how do we come into full bloom? Practice. Like all things, practice is key. When we are having a bad day, that is one of the most important days to be mindful of gratitude and its power. Keep a gratitude journal, like this one, close by and collect moments of gratitude. When you are having a bad day, open your journal and reflect on the beautiful moments that enlightened your soul. Remember how good it felt when you gave something so simple, yet in such large quality to the world. The key to keeping this flower nurtured, healthy, and strong in moments of struggle is to be grateful for what it is, rather than what it isn't.

It's a pattern of routine. Practice this act of simplicity, and I promise you, the life you live will change. You will open your eyes to the beauty around you that was there all along. Gratitude has a way of making the small wonders come into focus, making them appear bigger. Gratitude also has the power to make the big problems appear smaller.

Gratitude changed my life. My dad passed away when I was fifteen. I suffered years of loss, struggle, abandonment, and depression. I felt like I was missing so much in my life and felt so alone. Then I woke up one day, looked around and realized I had so much to be grateful for. It was all right there around me, but I needed gratitude as a focus to see that it was there all along. I may not have had the same people in my life, but I had God to thank for the people who were there. I took a step back and analyzed what I did have. I had a roof over my head, my health, and a bed. Then I took another, bigger step back, and saw the world for its beauty of purity and innocence. I felt gratitude for its simplicity. I would sit outside and watch the birds fly, I felt the wind as it blew through the trees, I felt the warmth of the sun, I appreciated the smell of rain. Slowly but surely, I felt this feeling of gratitude and appreciation. I knew that no matter what disappeared in my life, God would never deduct the beauty and innocence of nature. Then it hit me, the universe and its energy will never stop evolving, and all I can do is be grateful for what it is, and even for what it wasn't. I learned the hard way to be grateful, even for the times I struggled. I even learned to be grateful for the tears that I shed, because I knew it was all part of the process of acceptance and gratitude.

I truly believe that gratitude heals. It heals wounds in all of its forms. It's the cheapest medicine that can never do harm to you or anyone around you. Sometimes it can go unseen in society, but it's the one thing that will never die in this world or abandon you. It is always within reach. It's up to us to use gratitude to its advantage to change our perspective and even the world around us.

I wrote this poem as a tribute to gratitude and the strength it gives us to soar as high as we wish. Through the eyes of a butterfly, we can perceive gratitude in all things, especially change. They are living proof that when you embrace change, beauty spreads its wings and takes a leap of trust.

The Eyes of the Butterfly
Watch me soar in the sky above.
I land on your nose,
As a simple act of love.
Sweet like a rose.

The wind beats against my wings,
I have been through it all.
I survived the biggest storm last spring.
But I always get back up when I fall.

I was once wrapped in a cocoon.
Clouds by day, storms by night.
I counted my stars and thanked the moon.
The sun always came up, and life became bright.

I became patient.
I trusted the process.
I practiced appreciation.

I began to shed the excess.

You'll never know you can fly

until you spread your wings and try.

I took a leap and to my surprise,

I had turned into a beautiful butterfly.

My heart embraced the change,

My love leveled at magnitude.

Kindness traveled through my veins,

and with that, prevailed and defined gratitude.

With much love,

Talia

TALIA RENZO was bullied at a young age, tremendously in school, and her dad passed away unexpectedly. She was completely abandoned and without the support of a family. As she experienced great loss, it brought her to a higher appreciation for wisdom. Talia decided not to fall the same way as everyone else did through life's greatest trials. Instead, she took all of her pain and channeled it into passionate writing and pearls of wisdom.

She wrote her first book at sixteen years old and has taken to writing for her own healing and to share inspiration for others in need of love, healing, and wisdom.

Connect with Talia
Visit her Facebook page for more poetry, updates, and wisdom
Facebook @ taliarenzo

I am grateful for ...

Week 19

Miracles occur naturally as expressions of love.
The real miracle is the love that inspires them.
In this sense everything that comes from love is a miracle.

~ A Course in Miracles

ANGEL BOY

Back in the spring of 1991, my husband and I had plenty to be grateful for, the most important of which was two beautiful daughters: Laura, our biological child, and Amanda, who had come to us through the gift of adoption six years later. We also had our share of disappointments, including the loss of an anxiously awaited third child, a boy whose birth mother had changed her mind about the adoption. We had no way of knowing that a much bigger plan for us was in place, or that it would be set in place one ordinary evening as we sat in front of the TV.

20/20 was airing a segment on the orphans of Romania. The political leadership of the country and other cultural factors had collided, and these children – thousands of them had been caught in the middle. As this was the days before the internet and the twenty-four-hour news cycle, Americans might never have known of their plight; now, within a few short minutes, it had been brought to the forefront of our national consciousness. Before we knew it, my husband and I were booking our flights.

My son Joey was two years old when I saw him for the first time in Bucharest. He was developmentally delayed and malnourished. The movement of his eyes indicated a possibility of some neurological problems. I was told by the first physician who evaluated him to choose another child, as this little boy had many medical issues and would not develop normally. I listened to what the doctor said, then looked into Joey's eyes and knew I could not leave him behind. I loved him already and knew he was to join our family.

I then consulted another physician, who headed the Aids Hospital for Children in Bucharest. As I walked into his office, there was a sign that read: We have done so much for so long with so little, that we can now do everything with nothing.

I will never forget him. He examined Joey and undoubtedly saw everything that the other physician had noted. However, instead of trying to dissuade me, he simply looked at me and said, "He is your son, take him home and love him."

There would be many people who helped us during this process, especially Heather, our adoption facilitator. I was grateful to all of them. But I have the most gratitude for that physician. His words gave me the courage to know that my decision was the right one and was meant to be.

Throughout my son's life the challenges have been varied and many. Though he understands things quite well, he is non-verbal, which makes communication difficult. He has gone through periods of troublesome behavior, one of the toughest being running away. Joey loved to run from the house and we would need to call the police to locate him. We had multiple locks on the doors, but he would always get out. He was like a little Houdini, who, coincidentally, was from Romania as well! Eventually he outgrew this, only to begin destroying things around the house - furniture, lampshades, mattresses... the list went on and on. Now that Joey is an adult, I am filled with gratitude that he was kept safe – and that we lived in a city with plenty of furniture stores where we could restore our rooms!

There is a popular saying that it takes a village to raise a child. For a child with autism, this takes on an entirely new magnitude. The gratitude I feel for Joe's teachers and therapists over the years is beyond words. They always had the patience and perseverance to forge ahead and celebrate progress. I remember one teacher in particular, who would share her morning coffee with him when he was in high school as he had a hard time waking up. It is with a grateful heart that I remember his first speech therapist, who tirelessly worked with pictures and symbols to assist with Joe's reading. There were many wonderful assistants and respite workers who were instrumental in Joey's growth and development over the years. His assistant Liz always said he was the son that she never had. She called him "Angel Boy," but I consider her our angel, and I will be forever grateful for the love and support that she and her family gave to mine.

Then there were the people in our community who met Joey's fist bump or high five with a gentle smile. His intuitive nature always knew people who would be open to his greetings. Other times, these people accepted those difficult behaviors I mentioned, like the man in the restaurant pickup line who Joey ran up to and kicked in the shins. Horrified, I quickly ran up to the man and apologized. His response was a surprising one, "I have been beat up all day at work. That was nothing."

I have tremendous gratitude for my friends, especially other mothers who are walking this journey with me. Though often in the throes of their own challenges and heartbreak, these incredible women always took time to listen to me and offer support. They also shared with me their research on medications, diet, behavioral therapies, and many other therapeutic interventions. My friend Wendy encouraged me to seek out a program called SPRED that helps special needs children prepare to receive the sacraments in our church. Most importantly, these friends have helped me to honor my own feminine spirit and recognize my ability to nurture all of my children, mind, body and soul.

Joe's connection to spirit is so powerful. When he was young, a woman asked me if he watched TV. When I replied that he did not, she said, "Well, if you could see angels like he does, you would not be interested in watching TV either."

Joey has changed the trajectory of our entire family. He has two brothers and six sisters who love and support him, each in his or her own way. Since the day he came home with us, their lives have never been the same. Though it has not always been easy their minds and hearts have grown with the experience. It is one they will take out into the world and in some subtle yet powerful way and make it a better place.

We work together for the ever-growing consciousness and expansive views surrounding autism and all those with disabilities, including an awareness of and appreciation for the unique gifts and passions that they bring to the world. We recognize that every person - regardless of their challenges and diagnoses - deserves the opportunity to find purpose for their lives and be integrated into our communities.

The gifts Joey has brought to my life are without measure. Although there were times, I wished I could have done more for him, had more time for therapies and knew better how to reach him, I am so grateful to be his mother.

Temple Grandin, professor of animal sciences at Colorado State University and the first person to openly speak about life with autism, once stated, "The world needs all kinds of minds." I know firsthand the truth of these words, and I am deeply honored and grateful for being given the chance to be a part of Joey's world.

ANN BROWN is a registered nurse, certified intuitive and holistic healing practitioner specializing in the support of children on the wide spectrum of autism, with the inclusion of ADD, ADHD and Asperger's. In her work Ann utilizes healing touch, essential oils, nutrition (including whole food supplements), yoga as therapy and spiritual direction.

She also offers a complementary approach to health and healing to children and young adults facing emotional disorders, as well as their families. Her signature program, "Mystic Heart Healing," combines health and wellness consulting, energy medicine and spiritual companionship and direction.

Ann is the mother of nine children and five grandchildren, and has personal experience living and loving under the "spectrum umbrella."

Connect with Ann
ann@spectrumspirit.com
spectrumspiritualwellness.com

I am grateful for ...

Week 20

Joy is the simplest form of gratitude.

~ Karl Barth

FOREVER YOURS

It's Christmas Eve day, traditionally a day of preparation, festivities, and family. The typical northwest Christmas Eve scene includes a soft dusting of white snow and easily navigable streets. Although the roads are clear, parking lots and available spaces are filled with heaps of snowplowed blackened, dirty snow. Still snowing, oversized orange snowplows with enormous curled steel blades dominate crowded streets of hurried shopper's cars.

The temperature is slightly above freezing; the crisp and refreshing air chaps my lips. The one hundred fifty-mile trip through mountainous Montana, Idaho and eastern Washington typically involves a three-hour drive. Today, it's four. Ponderay, Idaho is always congested, especially the intersection of the new Starbucks and Walmart.

Near the Schweitzer ski hill, roads are especially hazardous, particularly in shaded areas. Last minute shoppers rush through Sandpoint toward larger shopping areas at Coeur d'Alene and Spokane. At Spokane Valley, burgeoning parking lots overflow with cars of every color.

Courageous Salvation Army bell ringers, wearing white gloves and Santa Claus suits, stand behind red metal cauldrons. Shared coins clank loudly, dropping into the kettle. Grateful bell ringers cheerfully open doors for passing shoppers.

I'm feeling a little anxiety, or is it excitement? Breathe. Maybe it's a bit of both. Locating Spokane, Washington's airport freight depot may be a bit of a trick. But first, an essential stop near the Northtown Mall. Sees Candy is a must. Their peanut brittle is the finest, candy caramelized perfection, and rum nougats, the perfect gift for my team and family. The line ahead of me is long but will be worth the wait. Small, pleasant conversations among customers are guaranteed. Large, old-fashioned black and white floor tiles, white uniforms and immediate, welcoming smiles imply old time hospitality. Sweet smells of holiday candy, rum nougat samples, plus red and gold gift wrapping with delicate gold elastic bow ties add to the perceived value. Two bulging Sees white shopping bags, double bagged, ensure there is one for everybody.

Traditionally, I purchase several additional boxes, later placing them anonymously inside cars, under Christmas trees or on doorsteps. My brother and sister-in-law, David and Diane, initiated the tradition many years ago. It is a Christmas I recall with particular fondness. Due to the expenses of building a new home, there was a shortfall of available cash. During their Christmas Eve visit, they covertly slipped gifts under our tree. On Christmas morning, we discovered special stuffed kittens for my girls, white knee-high stockings, cherry flavored Chapstick, a slightly perfumed makeup for me, plus chocolates. More than the gifts, I am grateful for the love, thoughtfulness, and unique holiday traditions shared with our families.

Glancing at my watch, I believe there is enough time for lunch. The Onion Restaurant is just a few blocks north of Northtown Mall. It's a perfect day for a bowl of French onion soup, salad and a warm, grainy wheat roll with sweet cream butter … healthy, tasty, and fast.

No one in their right mind would deliberately choose this day for long distance travel. Noticing a wave of energy again, I convince myself this is excitement.

"I intend to be in gratitude," I tell myself. With intention, touching my heart center, I quiet the nervous voice in my head. "This will be fun! It's an adventure."

It's chaos at the Spokane airport, provoked by late arrivals and weather delays. Finding a lone metered parking space, somewhat close to the information center, I pull in and feed the meter. My steps are hurried toward the airport entrance. At baggage claim, a camouflaged soldier retrieving duffel bags is rushed by her blonde, curly haired daughter.

"Mama! Mama, you're home!"

We all stop for a few seconds, sharing the moment.

As I find the circular information center, there is no distinct line. People rush up from all directions. The desk attendant, resembling a conductor, answers questions rhythmically without missing a beat.

"Will you direct me to the special package depot, please?"

"The buildings o're there, Miss. The tan building," he offers. "Next?"

I hesitate to bring it to his attention, but they're all tan! The narrow highway increases the odds of my finding the depot. Maybe this is it. Pulling in hesitantly, I search in vain for a sign.

The parking lot resembles a speedway. Brown UPS trucks and white FedEx vans rush by hurriedly. Good Heavens! It might be safer to park in the next lot. This is their busiest day of the year, and they're running out of time. With penetrating eyes, I look for a door ... surely there's a door. Circling the unmarked building, I pull on the handle of the first door I come to. It's locked. Steel gray, ice cold, and locked. My paperwork says 1:00. I'm right on time if I am at the correct building. Walking around the building in search of another door, I hear the first steel door open behind me. Maybe I can catch it quickly before it closes. Yes! I have a foot in the door.

The clerk is blonde, hair pulled tightly into a ponytail. Her dark blue uniform and silver badge resemble an officer's uniform. Rummaging through a clipboard full of bent cornered papers, she glances at me suspiciously.

"Hello, is this the special freight depot?"

Sizing me up, "Do you have your papers?"

Surrendering my purchase papers, airline forms, and driver's license, I feel butterflies.

"Wait right here."

It is a long few minutes. The walls are barren, gray painted 8"x8"x16" concrete blocks. The floors are slick, gray painted concrete. The counter is tall, with a worn out dingy white, scratched, exposed veneer. It is colder inside than outside. The Washington air is high in moisture. Breathing into my cupped, gloved hands, I see the vapor. Good heavens! It's cold in here! There are no windows, only gunmetal gray metal doors at opposite ends.

Bustling in the back, she emerges suddenly. Lifting a large green-hued turquoise fiberglass travel crate onto the counter,

"This one is yours," she said, stepping back.

Huddling bashfully in the corner is a woeful little soul, a perfect Eeyore.

The moment I laid eyes on him, he won my heart.

"Well come here, Sweetheart," unlocking the crate door, "Let's have a look at you."

Reaching inside, I find a resistant, round-bellied six-week-old puppy. Hind legs drag like skipping brakes as I lift him from the crate.

"My goodness! Look at you," I cooed. "All the way from Iowa."

Clearly embarrassed, he's a black and white, freckle-faced English Springer Spaniel with beautiful, look-away eyes. Cradling him at my chest, breathing my essence lightly into his face, I hear a long puppy sigh. Ahh! I am grateful for this moment. Unbuttoning the top of my coat, tucking him in, I conclude the paperwork. Holding him up, giggling at his little belly, I place his massive front paws over my shoulder.

"Let's go home."

His bright button eyes dance with delight as he tussles my long mahogany French braided hair with pinpoint puppy teeth. Playing out quickly, he buries his face between my neck and wool coat collar. Surrendering, he emits a second long, audible sigh, as if to say,

"I am forever yours."

BONNIE LARSON, Spiritual Mentor Practitioner & Bestselling Author.

Bonnie Larson is a Lay Minister, Reiki Healer, Healing Minister, Spiritual Mentor, Mind, Body Spirit Practitioner, Angel Prayer Practitioner, Heart Math Practitioner, Published Author, and Accomplished Business Executive.

She is a VIP Spiritual Leaders Top Pick 2018.

Bonnie is a life-long student of religion, science, and spirituality, also philosophy, history, and business. She is passionate about helping others achieve their highest possible potential.

Bonnie is a published author of various poems, prayers, meditation, and short stories.
Bonnie's book, Flying So High, epitomizes her philosophy. Appreciating and supporting the courage, greatness, and beauty in others, we are sure to develop these qualities within ourselves. Flying So High demonstrates combining talents while working in the spirit of cooperation leads to cohesive, harmonic, diverse societies.

Connect with Bonnie
flyingsohigh.com
bonnielarson.net
bonnie@bonnielarson.net

I am grateful for ...

Week 21

*As with all commandments, gratitude is a
description of a successful mode of living.
The thankful heart opens our eyes to a
multitude of blessings that continually surround us.*

~ James E. Faust

THE GRATEFUL HEART

My whole life I was told to say, "Thank You and "You are Welcome." In our family this was not a choice, it was expected. It wasn't until I was well into adulthood that I realized these words were not supposed to be rote responses, but said with meaning.

As I grew older, there were people other than family to whom I was to be thankful: friends, co-workers and even complete strangers who had helped me in various situations. I would say "Thank you," but rarely heard "You're welcome" in response. It was as if they knew I was just saying the words, not feeling them.

That all changed in my early twenties. While in my twenty-sixth week of pregnancy, I awoke at three a.m. one morning not feeling well at all. I had a backache, my stomach was bothering me, and worst of all, I had no idea what was going on. My husband was sleeping and not wanting to bother him, I ran a bath in the hopes that it would help. All that I kept thinking was, if this is what pregnancy is like, I don't like it one bit.

Within an hour, I was having so much pain I knew something was wrong. I tried to pull myself out of the tub but couldn't. I called out for my husband, but he was a sound sleeper and did not answer, so I started to yell for help. I could hear my husband jump out of the bed, then he came to the bathroom, clearly startled. "What are you doing?" he asked, "I have to work in the morning."

I started to cry and told him I was in pain and could not get out of tub. He held out his hand, and when he saw I could not even lift my arms to grab it, he bent down and lifted me out.

As I stood up my water broke. I was in labor, the baby's head was coming out, and I was terrified. Yet for the first time in my life I also felt truly grateful; I was so thankful my husband was there with me. I told him to go call an ambulance, and since we only had a corded phone at the time, he had to leave the room to make the call. He gently helped me to the bathroom floor and dashed out. A moment later I could hear him on the phone, yelling at the person on the other end of the line to hurry. He told them I was in labor, but he never mentioned how far along I was, or how far the labor had progressed. After a few very painful moments and a couple of little pushes, the baby was out and crying so softly, it was a sound that stays with me today. I started yelling at my husband to tell them to hurry.

I could tell the person on the phone was trying to assure him that the baby would be okay, and that help would be there soon. My husband hung up the phone and came into the bathroom, letting out a gasp when he saw me holding our son in the palm of my hand. He was only about ten inches long, but he was in the fetal position and continued the strained cry.

When the ambulance got there, I was filled with an indescribable feeling that I would later recognize as gratitude. I heard footsteps as the paramedics entered the bathroom. I could see the panic in their faces when they looked at the baby.

"Is it a boy or a girl?' one of them asked.

"A boy," I answered, then started trembling and crying uncontrollably.

The next few hours were like a nightmare: the paramedics got us to the nearest hospital, where we were allowed to watch them work on our son through a window. About two hours later, the doctor came out and told us they would be sending the baby to a specialty hospital forty miles away. He was going by helicopter; we would have to drive. I had just finished giving birth, but I couldn't think about that as we hurried to our car.

By the time my husband and I arrived at the other hospital, our son was in the neo-natal intensive care, surrounded by a team of doctors and nurses. They were attending to him with such compassion, I immediately knew we were in the right place, that they all knew what they were doing, and my heart once again filled with that feeling of gratitude I had never felt before.

This was one of the hardest nights of my young life. Just twelve hours after bringing him into the world, I had to say goodbye to my firstborn child. He was just not strong enough to survive this, and at that point I did not know that I could be either. As I looked around at the teary-eyed nurses and doctors who had worked so many hours to save his life, I knew that my life would never be the same. I was devastated, and at the same time I knew I had been given a gift: I had truly learned the meaning of gratitude.

Finding this gratitude would help me see things in a whole new light. It was no longer just words I was saying, it was about what was happening in the moment. On that awful day I had learned that others could be affected by things that happened in my life, and that they would be there for me and with me. I learned to take the time to acknowledge and feel what was happening around me in each situation. Being grateful was not only about appreciating the good things, but about showing gratitude for those who were there when you needed them most, during the hard times.

I believe that on the day I lost my son, God taught me a lesson, not only about loss and life, but gratitude for everything in my life. I now understood that not everything would turn out the way I thought it should, and I no longer expected them to. Instead, I had to choose to be grateful, regardless of the situation. Showing appreciation for all things in my life would help me through good times and bad.

Two years later, I was blessed with my daughter, who was healthy, beautiful and born on time. That incredible day let me know that not only was I finally ready to be a mother, but I would be able to teach her that saying "Thank you" is about much more than words. It's about a feeling.

HOLLY BIRD was born and raised in Tempe, Arizona. She has worked in marketing and sales, with a focus on education and speaking, and has a wealth of life experiences, from spiritual mentoring and marriage to gardening, cooking and traveling. One of her passions is sharing these experiences as a means of connecting with and helping others.

Connect with Holly
Hollysbirdnest.com
HollyBird@hollysbirdnest.com
Facebook @ hollysbirdnest
Facebook @ loveyourangels
Twitter @ hollyjbird

I am grateful for ...

Week 22

*Gratitude helps you to grow and expand;
gratitude brings joy and laughter into
your life and into the lives of all those
around you.*

~ Eileen Caddy

LEARNING GRATITUDE

It is easy to say, "I am grateful for....", and then leaving it up to generalities like, my family, my job, and my house, etc.; however, saying that phrase, just to say it, does not fully encompass gratitude. Learning to embody appreciation to the fullest capacity requires you to do a bit more work. I believe that the specifics of your thankful list need to be declared and one of the most important components to that is that you must embrace the emotion(s) that goes with it. Visualize that your heart is being filled with your favorite warm yummy beverage. That warm feeling you are encountering exudes a sense of joy, happiness, and a sense of security, even if it is only for seconds. That is gratitude.

When you begin to breathe in gratitude using all your senses, it will infect your body on a cellular level. The more gratitude you take in, the more you will encounter. As your supplementary intake increases, the more it will be released to the world, which in turn will brighten the day of other people. That is when it will come back to you exponentially. My advice is to start small and really embody the experience. We are always rushing to the finish line instead of taking in the view on the way.

My feelings of gratitude include the learning I have received from my greatest teachers, my children. It seems that every day I am learning something new from them. I have four children, two daughters and twin boys. My daughters are ages 32 and 16 and my twins are 27. Besides my children, my gratitude list includes that I am a retired Federal Law Enforcement Officer and that I am now able to do what I love and that is to help people. I have now been retired for almost four years. The skills I learned from working there for 25 years have been incorporated into my business. I am grateful for the opportunities that have been presented to me regarding my business. These opportunities have put my name and what I do into the public eye, not only in my own community but all around the world.

As I think about and write about these things that I am grateful for, I am using my senses to help bring that joy to my heart. One way I help to recreate those sensations when I am feeling a bit down or out of sorts is to utilize a Grateful Jar. When you are feeling that warm & fuzzy feeling inside work on capturing those feelings by writing them down on a piece of paper. Write the date along with a short descriptive narrative of what you were grateful for and why. Fold that piece of paper and put it in your Grateful Jar. When you need a quick pick-me-up, just randomly pick a piece of paper from your Grateful Jar and read it slowly. Remember what the situation was and really embrace the feelings of that experience. It will take you back to that situation and will put a smile on your face. Anything that you choose to put in your jar is perfect, just remember to be as descriptive as possible so when you pick that piece of paper in future months, you will be able to remember it as if it just happened.

Creating a Gratitude Board is another idea. This can be on the computer, like Pinterest or it can be an actual board. Utilize pictures from magazines and remember to write a short description based on what you are grateful for. Doing this will give you something to look at and experience daily. What a great reminder of all that you can and should appreciate daily. Expand your board as you feel guided, like weekly or monthly. Another suggestion is to allow a section of wall in one of the rooms you frequent often to be dedicated to your Gratitude Wall. It is where you can add inspirational quotes, pictures of family, drawings, and your own journaling. You can appreciate those moments as you enter that room. Have your family participate as well and talk about areas and situations in their life that they are grateful for.

Being grateful for your experiences will guide you to embrace the happiness you deserve. It will remind you what is truly important in your life. I believe and trust that when you start walking down that road, those petty areas in your life will begin to melt away and your stress level will diminish, which in turn will allow you to spread your happiness to those you encounter every day. Besides your immediate family, those you encounter at the grocery store, at the bank, at your child's school, and while walking in the mall will benefit from your bliss. Expressing that delight to others can done in the form of a smile. That smile may positively impact someone's day without you even realizing it; as a result, the ripple effect will start occurring. This will increase the energetic frequency throughout the world that leads to peace. Learning gratitude is a step you can take to not only embrace happiness in your own life, but to spread that happiness throughout the world.

MISTY PROFFITT is a Spiritual Life Coach, Mind, Body, and Spirit Practitioner, Angel Communicator, Intuitive/Psychic Medium, best-selling author, teacher, and speaker. She helps those who are struggling to find their purpose, so they can feel validated and obtain clarity. Misty started her business, Mystified Enlightenment, in 2016 and works with clients from all over the world.

Misty enjoys yoga, writing, and spoiling her grandchildren. She is married, has four children and four grand-children.

Connect with Misty
mistymthompson.com.

I am grateful for ...

Week 23

*When it comes to life the critical thing is
whether you take things for granted or
you take them with gratitude.*

~ G. K. Chesteron

GRATITUDE REFLECTIONS AND A STORY
TO SUSTAIN THE HURTING HEART
FROM ONE WHO HAS BEEN THERE

Gratitude Reflections and a Grateful Spirit. The first step in helping to sustain a recovering heart is to come, relax in the arms of the Lord your God, and allow Spirit to minister and comfort. Bask in gratitude for His love, grace and presence in daily life, and the holes made by loss shall be healed. Write of your reflections, and insight gained will guide your mind and heart with great grace. A grateful heart brings peace.

A Story of Gratitude. Gratitude will blossom as we worship with the Angels. Here is a little story of reminder, as the author experienced during a worship service.

She was finally able to attend worship again. There was a long period of time in which the grief for the loss of her husband overwhelmed her so strongly that she could not bear to go and cry her way through the service. But that was changing as time moved forward. Now she finds comfort in the presence of her church family and her related family. She never thought she would once more find companionship with her follow worshippers but this day—here she was, gathering with the other worshippers. Gratitude bubbled around in her inner woman, rising to the surface as the music was about to begin.

The back of the wooden bench felt hard against her back; she shifted positions trying to relax. All was quiet within the sanctuary; the congregation waited for what had come to be one of the most anticipated parts of the Sunday morning service. The young pianist was about to play.

She watched as he closed his eyes and the soft tinkling of the melody began — gentle, reverent, hauntingly beautiful. She closed her eyes, too, letting the music flow over her from head to toe; the notes transported her to a Heavenly place, where the music was alive with the vibration of praise.

Opening her eyes, she was startled as a vision began, and she observed notes rising from the oaken piano. Multi-colored notes — not the black notes as seen on a piece of sheet music, but colorful, floating and dancing notes of all sizes and shapes. She watched the notes rising into the air around the piano. The notes moved together in a rhythm straight from the young pianist's heart and mind. Their rhythm synchronized with the melody his fingers played on the keys.

And then she heard it — a soft whisper sound. She looked about the quiet sanctuary for the source of the sound. Around the young pianist, angels were gathering among the colorful notes. Forming a circle around him, they began to sway with hands raised to their Father in worship. Soon the circle started to move, slowly, in sequence with the musical phrasing. Sometimes they bent in prayer and awe. Sometimes they were spinning with joy as the colorful notes encompassed them. Sometimes they twirled painting a vibrant whirlwind of flashing and color and wings and notes. The notes, the angels and the sound all blended into a holy dance before the altar of the Lord.

The intensity of the music built, as did the emotions of the dance. Quickly the angelic worshippers began to move past the young pianist and into the sanctuary. The beat of his song became stronger and stronger. His fingers running up and down the keyboard caused a frenzied response. They moved up and down the aisles of the sanctuary spreading flashing, feathered wings over the heads of the earthly worshippers. For several minutes the intense, vibrant worship continued as the wind of Spirit meshed the music and angelic activity into a dance of praise and gratitude.

Suddenly, the music dropped speed and tenor. The altar beneath the stained-glass picture of Christ overlooking the sanctuary, filled with angelic worshippers, their wings folded in reverence, their heads bowed. The Spirit of the Lord once more, blew His soft presence over the worshippers, angelic and human. A holy hush quieted all present.

Ever so gradually the worshiping angelic host moved back around the young piano player. His music continued to soften in pace and reverence; lovingly they placed their wings on his shoulders. The vibrant notes began piling up throughout the sanctuary, like brilliant fall leaves, creating a carpet of color.

She bowed her head in prayer, feeling awed by the scene of vibrant worship she had been allowed to witness. She had shared a glimpse of Heaven and knew that this sanctuary was Holy ground, anointed ground, ground now prepared for the congregation to enter the presence of the Lord. Her mind went to the Bible verse in Psalms that teaches us to enter His gates with thanksgiving and His courts with praise. Knowing now she was included in those ancient instructions and not alone as she recovered from her grief. Tears of gratitude filled her eyes, threatening to spill over onto her cheeks. But these tears were different, not tears of grief she had shed so often. These were tears from a healing heart—tears of thanks and peace. She was encompassed by gratitude and the knowledge of how much we are all loved by Heavenly Father.

Words of Gratitude from God's Word. Steep your soul in the encouragement that comes from God's Word.

I thank you, Lord, and with all the passion of my heart I worship you in the presence of angels! Heaven's mighty ones will hear my voice as I sing my loving praise to you! I bow down before your divine presence and bring you my deepest worship as I experience your tender love and your living truth …

~ Psalm 138 1-2 (TPT Edition)

Spirit Sings a Song. Listen with the ears of your heart to the inner voice of Spirit bringing encouragement and joy. Imagine with gratitude the swirl of angelic host and notes embracing your entire being.

For the Lord, your God does not depart from you. When you are sad, and you hold grief and fear in your hands, lift them in praise. Do not think that the notes of love and the sounds of heaven are not welcoming your presence. The touch of love on your head, the feel of spiritual heat in your raised hands and the presence of grace upon your bowed head are always with you. We know that you have felt bereft in days past, but go forward, a step at a time. Wipe your tears on the hem of your Christ's robe. Allow the love we feel for you to fill your broken heart, calming your spirit. Gratefully remember the assurance that life will continue is being affirmed. It shall be as planned, for you are a child of the Living One, the God who counts the hairs on your head and saves your tears in a bottle. So, come to our gates with a grateful heart, with great thanksgiving, and a knowing that even in sadness all will vibrate with the joy of the Lord. Pause in our presence, and gratefully acknowledge that you are not alone.

~ The Voice of Spirit—Author's Journal

A Prayer of Gratitude for the Day. Help us this day Father to worship you as the angels do, joyously and full of the gratitude for your grace and presence in the minutia of our lives. We uphold our grateful hearts to you that your mighty love will fill us on our journey into the future. Thanks, and praise be yours forever.

Speak Gratitude Always. It is taught that what we speak out we bring about. Speak loudly of your gratitude and sing your praises loudly no matter the circumstances. Then wait. Wait. Wait. All will be brought about in His time and your grateful heart shall be made whole.

May grace, peace, and joy be yours now and in all the days to come. Written for you, with gratitude and love.

MARGARET-MAGGIE HONNOLD is a registered nurse and health educator living in a small midwestern town with her two Basset Hounds. Her first book, The Cloisonné Heart: A Memoir of Love was published in 2017. The memoir of caring for her late husband who died of complications from Alzheimer's Dementia, it's full of encouragement and love for others walking that path. Awarded a Finalist Position in the 2018 International Book Awards competition, it was a No.1 best seller on Amazon.

Her blog, The Art of Continuing Anyway, addresses aging, loss, dating, health and the humor of growing old. When not writing, she can be found around the countryside with her camera, shooting images for inclusion in her coffee table/poetry books, wall prints and original cards all available on her website.

Since retiring she serves on the Kibbe Museum Board, the Hancock County Humane Society Board and as elder for her church. Visit her website to read her blog or order her other books, prints, and cards.

Connect with Margaret
margarethonnold.com
machonnold@outlook.com
Facebook @ margarethonnold

I am grateful for ...

Week 24

If you concentrate on finding whatever is good in every situation, you will discover that your life will suddenly be filled with gratitude, a feeling that nurtures the soul.

~ Rabbi Harold Kushner

POLISHED THROUGH THE PAIN

No one tells you how the story will end, like watching a movie; you guess, assume and conjure up your own outcome that makes the most sense to you. So many movies leave us puzzled, perplexed and bewildered, wondering how could the scriptwriter think the audience would leave the theater satisfied with such an ending? You know what I'm talking about, the "What just happened?" "The ending sucks" kind of movies.

Yet life smacks us with these endings to the stories we are living more often than we want to view; instantly you look down and see your heart is in the palm of your hand, you are void of air, and you wonder how you will insert your heart back into your chest.

This was me one year ago, when an instant message asking me for my phone number changed the space of my reality, a phone call to a hospital hundreds of miles away and a voice on the other end speaking the unimaginable, "Your son was in a motorcycle accident, we gave him CPR for an hour but ..." BUT??? There is no but! Shut up, stop talking to me, you are not real, this is not the way this story ends!

As I turned into a mist in my kitchen, I unconsciously handed the tainted voice on the phone to my husband, and the vapor I had now become reappeared outside, screaming his name "Josiah, Josiah, Josiah, where are you, where are you??" Since I had no legs, the ground was my only refuge. Laboring to breathe I could hear a crackling from my hand that now held my heart, shredded.

The earth had shifted, spontaneously expanding my understandings that had vanished.

One by one love began to arrive - siblings, aunts, uncles, father and friends - each one entering with their hand dripping with the shreds of not only their heart but mine as well. Love has a unique dialect in a crisis and had advised them to hold a piece of mine. As each one of my beautiful children, relatives and friends managed to find my mist, our shreds blended until only one heart could be felt, "HIS."

One by one I gathered back the ribbons of my heart from theirs, this is my enigma and I needed every ribbon if I was going to survive this unimaginable alteration in the script and not just go with him, which momentarily teetered my thoughts.

How one day can alter perception like no other day has the possibility of doing, leaving you with more questions and no answers.

What do I do with the tear stained shreds that were once a heart, how do I reshape it and place it back in its proper position, what choice do you have when you had no choice?

All I had believed withered into the unstable earth my weakened bones now lay upon.

I am now unmolded clay on the sculptor's wheel, but how do I mold and create the next part of my present moment when I am a clay-less vapor? How do I surrender to the sculptor to mold me and move me in the direction I will become, the creation that only dark despair creates?

Grief has a way of sliding through you like no other emotion, shape shifting the current of your DNA. I felt like a moment was too distant to wander to, I believed I was broken beyond human recognition and that this was going to be my remaining existence.

When you are shredded, however that comes to be, you have a choice. You can absorb, digest and become - or you can stay defeated, which silences healing and secrets the re-scripting of this docudrama you are now living.

A friend asked me, "What is the gift he left you?" which challenged the alignment of my mind. So I began to question the gift in the shreds, in the ribbons of my heart, in the vaporized clay. I asked myself, What form do you choose to become, and how will you recalculate, reevaluate and respond to this act in your movie? I am now in the scene where I am faced with life at its rawest expression of cruelty, at least this is my initial perception ... this path feels wrong, blurred with deception, the earth is lying to me without words, and if this is not how it's supposed to end, then I am not at the ending, I am at a pause - an intermission where the actors realign and relationships redefine, including mine with Josiah ...

There it was, LOVE. Love appeared again, now in the vexed eyes of my children, "Will she stay, or will she go?" There was no way I was leaving them, I could feel the two worlds merging, how do I stay with him and be here with them?

My breath now bleeding, I sang out. "Josiah, it has been too many days, too many quiet moments. My labored breath awaits your voice, this void with no end, awaiting tears that perch my soul."

With ink still wet and without warning, I heard him! "Oh, Mother of this earth, I am with you, I hold your heart from here, stronger than I could when there, it is I that perch your soul."

His ginormous Spirit reminding me that he had me, that his presence had just changed form, that he was happy, healthy, healed and whole now, and that he would guide my way, our way, maybe your way.

I honestly can't give you a time frame when I reappeared in my body, I am sure I am not all there now, quite possibly, I never will be, I like the place in-between - the merge - but what I have come to know is I can't be there, unless I am here. Unless I live in Love, I won't be able to transmute this pain, which is Love on the deepest level.

We have all loved and lost, we have all carried the shreds and gathered the ribbons.

To say I am grateful doesn't feel right, but it doesn't feel wrong, just the mere fact that he chose me, that I had him in my body and that his magical being loved me, I am humbled. Gratitude seems too faint an expression.

If you were to ask me, "Raina, if you knew this was part of the script, would you say yes again?" I would answer, "Yes, a million times Yes! Yes, to loving him, yes to knowing him, yes to the privilege of being his mother, yes to the magic that is Josiah," and as my tears stain these pages, I say, "Yes, for the gift he gave me was himself, and I am beyond grateful."

Now I have form again, and I am being sculpted into something other than what I once was. My ribbons lay upon the sculpture differently yet uniquely still mine - repurposed. And though it may take beyond this lifetime to see the polished performance from this movie, to see the glossy finish, I willingly say, Yes, polish me Spirit, polish me Angels, polish me Josiah.

Let me be Love, let me be light and let me honor you in my movie, because it's not over.

To love is our greatest gift, to be Love is even greater.

Will you gather the ribbons, will you embrace your enigma, and will you rise with me and call on love to show you the gift? There are some pains so great that others fade in comparison. Choose to be polished, even if you can't see that you shine, someone else can. I can.

My Heart, My Soul, My Spirit, My Life will never be the same.

It will be Stronger.

Because of Josiah.

RAINA IRENE is a Heart, Soul, Spirit Practitioner and the owner of Beauty, Strength & Healing Inc. She is a Licensed Esthetician and holds multiple certificates in Holistic Health,

Spiritual Work and Emotional Healing. When she's not working, you can find Raina out on her mini ranch with her husband, hanging with her kids, grandkids and the animals.

Raina's Eclectic and Spiritual diversity enables her to tap into your unique needs, supporting and guiding you to clarity and connecting you with your own healing energies. She blends her Esthetics with Reiki, Essential Oils and Intuition; holds Healing Circles with the emphasis on Inner Wisdom and Understanding Grief. She educates from a heart of experience.

With two Siblings, Parents and now Son in Spirit, Raina has committed to sharing that our bonds continue, Love is forever... all you have to do is Believe and you will see.

Connect with Raina
Facebook @ GypsyRaina.Irene
Facebook @ gypsyraina
Join her Facebook group @ BeautyStrengthHealing

I am grateful for ...

Week 25

We delight in the beauty of the butterfly,

but rarely admit the changes it has gone

through to achieve that beauty.

~ Maya Angelou

SHOWING UP TO SHINE

Showing up for myself wasn't easy at first. In fact, for years it felt downright selfish. I had always put myself at the bottom of my own list and liked to blame others or circumstances "beyond my control" for my being there. You know, things like family issues; being too busy; stressing over what would happen or regretting past mistakes; looking for answers outside myself instead of listening to my own guidance; hiding behind the mask of "I'm so strong, I can handle anything;" and the big one - diminishing my light so others would not be uncomfortable (or so I would not be uncomfortable). My thoughts ran on a constant loop of it, "It's easier to just keep my mouth shut;" "I can 'fix' anyone or anything;" and "What will everyone think?"

When I was young, children, especially girls, were to be seen and look pretty but not be heard, put others' needs before their own, be polite and wait at the back of the line and accept whatever was left. Wants, desires, and dreams were for someone else – someone special. And whatever you do, Do Not Show Your Emotions. Vulnerability was not tolerated. I grew up believing it was easier to be a people-pleaser than to go against what someone else thought. I spent my teen years and early adulthood exhausted from going from one situation to the other, making sure everyone's expectations of me were met. I had to make sure everyone was happy, right? What would happen if everyone didn't like me? Working really hard and doing everything I "should" would make me liked and revered by everyone, right?

I looked everywhere for approval, everywhere except inside. I spent most of my energy trying to appear like I had it all together. Of course, my hair was always fixed, my makeup was always on and I was always dressed in stylish clothes. I didn't dare let anyone see me if I didn't pass my own inspection, until my look said, "I'm confident and I know it." But while on the outside I appeared calm, cool, and collected, my internal voice cried out for love and belonging. My "perfection mask" kept me from forming the close, loving relationships I longed for.

It has taken a long time, but I now realize those years of sadness and hurt contained many blessings. I've learned that it's not what I experience but what I tell myself about the experience that shapes my life and who I become. I have the power to see that everything happens not to me, but for me. I've also learned that what others think of me is none of my business. These blessings remind me to stay on my own life path and let everyone else do the same. My heart is full of gratitude for embracing these blessings!

I've always had this quiet voice inside saying, you have much to share, you can show people how to shine. The problem was, I thought my shine was on the outside, and though this is part of it, I now know the real shine comes from doing the inside work. Now my inside matches my outside!

My journey of self-love and putting myself first is far from finished. As part of my commitment to this journey, I have daily reminders to show up for myself.

♥ Showing up for me is being vulnerable; no more masking my feelings for fear of being weak or being judged by myself or anyone else.

♥ Showing up for me is taking full responsibility for what I create and have created in my life. There is no one to blame, not even myself. I look at my life experiences through the eyes of love and forgive myself and others.

♥ Showing up for me is shining my light and being the greatest expression of who I am. No more hiding behind the fear of what others will think. I no longer hold back my love.

♥ Showing up for me is taking time to read, meditate, and reflect. I start each day with intention, so I'm filled with purpose and miracles all day.

♥ Showing up for me is letting everyone take care of their own life, in their own way. I know that we all have what we need inside to do that.

♥ Showing up for me is saying yes to the things I want to do and no to the things that don't resonate with me. I do a quick check-in with my hand on my heart and listen to my inner guidance. That inner guidance is always working for my highest and greatest good. I trust!

♥ Showing up for me is being in the present moment, not fretting over the past or anxious about the future. My power is here in this present moment. I can create the life I want!

♥ Showing up for me is trusting the process of the Universe. I no longer need to know everything before I move forward. One step at a time, the Universe has my back!

♥ Showing up for me is knowing I am deserving of the life I dream of. I have everything I need to create the life I desire!

♥ Showing up for me is telling myself every day that I AM ENOUGH!

♥ Showing up for me is releasing the fears that kept me still for so long. I move in the direction of love, step by step, moment by moment.

♥ Showing up for me is encouraging others to show up for themselves. I now have much to share. My gratitude overflows!

♥ Showing up for me is sharing a part of myself in this book. I am forever filled with gratitude for this opportunity and for the many teachers in my life. Thanks for helping me shine!

JUDY JAMES has been a hairstylist for 37 years. During this time, she has held numerous roles, including salon owner, educator with a major haircare brand, mentor, and state board examiner. She has also continued her own education in order to keep current with trends.

When asked what has kept her in the industry all these years, Judy says she loves coloring, cutting and styling, but her real passion has always been connecting with and helping people. To this end, Judy has volunteered her services, giving hundreds of haircuts to hospice patients, residents of homeless and women's shelters, and at numerous cut-a-thons.

Most of all, Judy is excited to continue on her journey of self-love and to share her experiences and connect with others on the same path.

I am grateful for ...

Week 26

Gratitude is the fairest blossom which

springs from the soul.

~ Henry Ward Beecher

BARBARA IN A BOX

After my mother passed, my sisters and I were going through everything in her cabin located in the beautiful mountain community of Idyllwild, California. Our next task was even more daunting; go through the all the stuff accumulated in her large two-car garage. In her defense, some of that "stuff" she'd been storing belonged to us. We were almost at the end of this huge task when I spotted a square, long box on the top of one of the built-in shelves. I got a ladder and pulled it down; it was white with a label on the outside.

"Hey, I found one of Mom's recipe boxes," I said, which caused my sisters to come running. My mother may have been a pack rat, but she was also the one who held the family recipes and history at her fingertips. With everyone gathered around me I slowly opened the box, surprised by not recipes, but by a clear plastic bag with a white powdery substance that looked like flour.

"That's not recipes," I said.

We just stood there staring at it. I couldn't figure out why anyone would hold on to a box with a bag of flour inside of it.

It was like a light bulb went on. I saw the eyebrows raise on each of my sisters as recognition caught up with them.

"Oh my God," I said.

On the card on the outside of the "recipe box" was typed a name, Barbara Lightner.

"Does anyone know who this is?"

We were dumbfounded and then horrified. My paranormal writer's mind went to a million absurdly awful places and possibilities about who she was and how she had possibly ended up in my mother's garage. I would like to say that we reverently placed her back on the shelf, but we ended up sitting on the grass, rolling with laughter, tears streaming down our faces. Then I started to feel a little guilty for laughing while I held a stranger's ashes in my hands. At least I had a name. How could this possibly be? Who is she? And more importantly, why in the world would our mother not tell us anything about her?

A year before my mother's passing, our stepfather, Phil passed. At the time, they were living in Moreno Valley, California, and before that, San Diego, California. It had been at least eight years since they'd lived in the cabin full time. Following his death, my mother wanted to move back to Idyllwild. My sisters and I didn't know anyone in Idyllwild, although we gathered there for holidays and special occasions. I met a few people when they came to see my mother, and to offer their support and help.

After my mother passed, my sisters and I decided to sell the cabin. I would stay in Idyllwild until it sold, which meant that when my sisters left, Barbara stayed with me. It was disturbing to me that Barbara was in that box, with no clue as to who she was or how to get her ashes to her family. I felt a nudge, an internal push to do something. I know that push, it's always right, and it's insistent until I listen.

Several restless days later, I took action. The only person I knew was our realtor, and I started there. I walked into her office, with Barbara in my hands and placed her on Marge's desk, "Do you know who this is?" I asked.

Marge never skipped a beat. "I have no idea, but Phil was a volunteer firefighter for many years. Maybe check there."

"Can I help you?" handsome firefighter number one asked. I have a theory that all firefighters are handsome. His looks helped prove my theory.

"Yes, thank you." I told him about Barbara and sat her up on the counter.

There was an awkward silence. It never even occurred to me that someone might raise an eyebrow at me carrying around ashes. However, I was on a mission, and I had the most intense feeling that Barbara did not want to be in that box.

"I think I remember hearing something about this. Why don't you come back tomorrow morning? The old-timers come in about 8:00 a.m. for coffee, you can ask around."

The next morning at 8:00 a.m. sharp, Barbara and I arrived at the fire station where there was, in fact, a table full of old-timers having coffee. Handsome firefighter number two introduced me, and I told them about Barbara. When the laughter subsided, one of the old-timers spoke, "I remember this. Phil and his buddy were supposed to take her remains up in his plane and scatter her ashes, but then Phil found out it was illegal." I knew enough about my stepfather to know how respectful he was about rules and laws.

"Do you know who Barbara is?" I asked.

There were only shakes of the head and a few of them saying, "Sorry."

According to the date typed on the outside of Barbara's box, she passed seventeen years earlier; predating my mother and stepfather's marriage by five years. Did they take her with them every place they moved to, or did she sit on that top shelf of the garage all this time? My feeling that Barbara needed to have a forever home continued to grow stronger.

A few days later, Marge called to tell me my mother's home sold. I was determined that Barbara would not be making any more trips. I had done everything humanly possible, except hiring a private detective—which was still an option and on my radar for next steps. I finished getting the house ready for the new owners and headed over to the local nail salon. I was telling Barbara's story to my manicurist when I heard laughter coming from a shadowed corner of the room, "Barbara would have loved this story," a female voice said. She introduced herself and passed along kind words about Phil and my mother.

"Barbara and Phil were very close friends. She used to tease him all the time about being a master procrastinator," she said.

After discovering who Barbara was and why her ashes were in my mother's garage, I realized that I had been on a divinely guided journey. Not only to uncover Barbara's mystery, but to appreciate why my mother, stepfather, and Barbara loved it there so much. My mother and deceased loved ones and Barbara were behind it all, guiding me to realize that life continues even when we are divided by physics. It's been many years since that happened. That experience continues to warm my heart and fill me with gratitude.

Barbara had no family, and no one to take her ashes. For me, there was only one thing left to do: honor her choice. I called a friend of mine who was an ordained minister. We took Barbara to the highest, most beautiful cliff we could find, said some words for her and wished her well, releasing her over the mountain community that was her home and family.

CAROLAN DICKINSON is a psychic medium, angel communicator, teacher, and author of the book, Walking with the Archangels (Amazon, 2016). Her essay, The Magic of Healing with the Archangels, is featured in the anthologies, Spiritual Leaders Top Picks (Visionary Insight Press, 2017), and 111-Morning Meditations-Start Your Day with Intention, (SDJ Productions, 2017), an Amazon #1 Best Seller.

Her first love is helping people learn to connect and build a relationship with their Spiritual Team and to develop their own gifts and talents. She teaches classes and workshops both in person and online at Udemy on Archangels, Angel Card Reading, Intuitive Development, Usui Reiki, and Mediumship.

She devotes her time doing psychic medium and past life readings for clients. In her free time, you will find her reading, in a yoga class, or walking and talking with the archangels.

Connect with Carolan
carolandickinson.com

I am grateful for ...

Week 27

It is not joy that makes us grateful,

it's gratitude that makes us joyful.

~ David Steindl-Rast

GRATITUDE FROM GRIEF

March 1, 2006. I sat alone under a wide-open blue sky on a beautiful spring afternoon. The sun was a powerful fireball in the sky warming my already hot, raw cheeks and forced me to squint and close my tired eyes. It was hot, I broke a sweat and could feel the nervous energy take over my entire body, but I still tried to feel the beauty of the sun on my hot, flushed cheeks. I knew I wasn't alone on that bench, I could feel him closer to me than he'd ever been, and yet I felt the most alone I had ever felt in my life. Somehow in my infinite sadness and brokenness I still felt gratitude in my soul for the sun and its warmth and the beauty of that blue sky. How was that even possible?

Gratitude is funny isn't it? Not 'ha-ha' funny, but ironically funny like Alanis Morissette's song. Not the act of gratitude, but the concept of gratitude can be so tricky to grasp. I know I have found myself asking if it's even possible to express genuine gratitude when I'm in the middle of one of life's storms. How can I possibly feel grateful for anything when I want to throat punch the world and everyone I encountered in it? I used to think that everything had to be right in my world in order to express gratitude and that gratitude was reserved for special occasions like Thanksgiving, Christmas or my wedding anniversary. I don't know why I thought of gratitude this way. What would have ever made me think that gratitude needed to be reserved for the perfect situation or for a special occasion?

Eighteen days earlier after a fabulous girl's weekend, I arrived home to witness Trevor gingerly getting out of our truck; one boot on, one boot obviously missing. Our usually pristine quad looking worse for wear. My girls' weekend bliss and relaxation instantly left my body and mind. I immediately charged at him asking a million questions. All he could say was "I think I should go to the hospital". So off we went.

Who knew that that single visit would lead us down the path we ended up on?

Those eighteen days ended up being the longest and shortest days of our lives. Watching Trevor struggle with the pain, swelling and discomfort in his foot and calf along with unexplained shortness of breath, tiredness and an unrelenting cough was unbearable at times. My heart sank every time he had to sit down to catch his breath or his toes turned another shade of blue. Ignorance is not bliss. Ignorance allowed us to carry on with everyday life, it allowed me to sit at my desk and happily book a family their dream vacation while my beloved unknowingly prepared himself to die.

Gratitude is the light at the end of the tunnel, sometimes that light is dim and small and feels a million miles away and sometimes it is big and bright and so close that you can reach out and grab it. It's in those moments when it seems so far away and so pointless, that I strive even harder and dig even deeper, to feel the gratitude I have for the life I have been given. Every experience, every lesson, every heartbreak, every failure, every stumble, every ounce of grief and rage and sadness I have ever felt has led me to feel more gratitude daily. If I had not been given this life to live, I would not be the woman I am today. I would not feel and experience love as deeply as I do, I would not see the beauty that I do in every one of God's creations, I would not appreciate the adventures and daily musings that I do. Life would simply go on around me, I would not live it as loudly as I do. My heart is full because I find reasons to feel grateful.

Remember in junior high when you approached a group of girls who were talking intently and as soon as you entered their circle, the conversation stopped, and they all had 'that look' on their face? You instantly knew you were their topic; your heart sank, and your cheeks flushed. That's a feeling I'd like to forget from that day, a memory that I'd like to wipe clean. Walking up to the triage desk to tell the nurse who I was and ask where my husband was; I suddenly felt fourteen again. Every nurse in the place stopped for a moment, their eyes dropped as they awkwardly tried to avoid making eye contact with me. All at once I was confused, annoyed and growing more and more pissed off. Awkwardly I asked, then I asked again, then I demanded that someone start explaining what was going on.

That room that we've all seen in movies and created in our heads from reading about it in books, is shockingly accurate. Stale. Hospital green. No windows and a garbage can in the corner by the door. A table with nothing but a phone and a box of tissues on it, two chairs on one side, one chair on the other. This is where I was led, with a gentle yet forceful hand in the small of my back. In walked the doctor that had treated Trevor eighteen days earlier. You can imagine my reaction, I'm sure. The words finally came out of his mouth: "We did everything we could, but your husband did not make it, we are very sorry". So now there I was, twenty-eight years old, alone and now, a widow.

My beloved taken out of this world by a silent killer that lurked in his body for eighteen days. Official cause of death: Cardiac Arrest from a Pulmonary Embolism. Unofficial cause of death: Ignorance. My final memory at that hospital that day was the sun on my face and a wide-open blue sky. I was grateful to be out of that room, away from the tilted heads and sad faces. Grateful to be alone and at the same time incredibly sad to be that alone.

As years passed my life was ruled by anger, anxiety, rage and sadness all the while, new love had blessed me. Happiness and joy had returned, and adventures soothed my soul. Life was a constant struggle. I had been handed every reason not to live in gratitude; my husband had died, friends betrayed me, family judged me and refused to support me. I had been taken advantage of, stolen from and lied to by people who promised to be there for me. My heart has broken a thousand times since that sunny spring day on that bench. Somehow through all of it, one message found its way onto my heart and into my soul; Be Grateful.

It baffles me now to think that I didn't know how to implement gratitude in a simple everyday way. Maybe it was so difficult to grasp because of its ridiculous simplicity. Maybe it was just something that needed to be practiced, like learning to play the guitar. It was nearly seven years later when another pivotal moment in my life forced my thoughts and ideas around gratitude to shift. I came to know that I didn't need to be happy every day in order to express gratitude in my life but rather, the more I expressed gratitude for my life, the more happiness I would find. That awakening changed everything for me, my whole life tilted on its axis.

Every day I get to feel love and give love, my body allows me to move and experience adventure. I have a beautiful marriage filled with love, fun, understanding, passion and friendship. I have talents that God gave me that allow me to reach people daily with my story. I am healthy. I have friendships that run deep. I get to live surrounded by natural beauty. I have a roof over my head and food in my belly. I get to pay bills and have a bank account. I have in-laws who love me unconditionally. I have had my fur baby Harley to love and be loved by for seventeen years. My list of reasons to feel grateful is endless and it continues to grow despite the challenges and traumas that have come into my life. I was faced with a choice many years ago, to either focus on the sadness and the things I could not change, or to find the good and choose happiness. I chose happiness, I hope you do too.

ROBYN OSTLUND had survived a laundry list of traumas before she turned 30. There is a good reason she has been described as tenacious, strong, confident, caring, motivated and a fighter - because she had to be. Being a God loving, red headed Taurus has definitely contributed to her success in life and business.

Robyn lives a simple life nestled in BC's mountains with her husband and feisty fur baby, Harley. Robyn's special variety of very bold, educational and humorous inspirational messages about life, health and fitness can be found in her blogging work, social media and from stage.

If your life could use some witty inspiration, a simplified and systemized approach to health, nutrition and fitness along with a daily sprinkling of glitter and no excuses attitude, then you're going to want to dive into the Deliberately Simple Life community with Robyn and her tribe.

Connect with Robyn
Facebook @ robyn.ostlund
Facebook @ ignitedhealth
Facebook group @ DeliberatlySimpleLife
ignitedhealth.com
Instagram @ the_real_robyno
Instagram @ ignitedhealth

I am grateful for ...

Week 28

What hurts you, blesses you.

Darkness is your candle.

~ Rumi

THE GAIN FROM THE PAIN

One would never think that a child's darkest moments could one day be something to appreciate, yet this is exactly what happened to me. One would never think that someone who had endured the trauma of childhood sexual abuse would say they are grateful for this abuse, yet this is how I feel. I know you probably read that sentence, then read it again, thinking there must be some mistake, that I had written it wrong, and if not, that something must be really wrong with this picture. How can anyone feel gratitude for something so dark? First of all, let me tell you that getting to this point was not easy, but a very long, very painful journey. However, when I did get there, I realized that from my abuse I had learned three very powerful lessons.

The first lesson relates to that uneasy feeling you probably got when you read that I had been sexually abused. Most people grow uncomfortable when sexual assault is mentioned, especially when the victim is a child, and especially if they have not experienced it themselves. This discomfort shows on their faces; they can't make eye contact and they fumble for the right words to say. But what really gets me is how much this topic gets swept under the rug, as if it didn't exist. This is actually what happed in my family. When a victim summoned the nerve to tell what happened, they found that no one wanted to talk about it, no one wanted to go to the authorities; instead, they covered it up in order to protect the family name. What happens when you bury a secret? The abuser is never punished and continues to hurt other innocent children. It becomes a festering wound, passed down from generation to generation.

I grew up believing this topic was off limits. Even years after I had moved far away from my family, I still found it extremely difficult to talk about the abuse. Though I wanted to confide in someone, I didn't think anyone would want to listen. That's when I realized that sexual abuse was not just a secret in my family, but in our society in general. I found myself wanting to rebel against this taboo, and to let light into what had been a very dark place. By this time, I had done a lot of inner work, and I could immediately tell when someone had not yet arrived at that point. It was from this place of intuitive knowing that I began to reach out to and truly connect with others, especially my fellow survivors.

The second lesson I learned from the abuse was how amazing my body truly is. For years I never understood why others remembered their childhood so clearly while my memory had huge gaps in it. I had only one memory of the abuse, though it had actually happened many times. I never tried to uncover other memories, in fact I was trying my best to forget the one I did have. It was of no use, though; this particular incident was burned in my mind, and I hated my body for it. Then, one day, I finally dug deeper into the experience. Through journaling, I realized that my body had not betrayed me, as I previously believed; instead, it had been protecting me. That day my body did what it could to try to stop the abuse, and indeed, it turned out to be the last time it ever happened. When I realized this, I was finally able to release the anger I had held onto for so long. When I finally took the time to sit and talk to my body and get to the bottom of my feelings, I realized it had not been acting as my enemy, but my friend all along.

The third and possibly the most powerful lesson I learned was, that I have something of value to offer the world. Surviving sexual abuse and coming out the other side has given me the tools to help others who went through or are going through the same thing. I know what the experience can feel like - I know the guilt a victim feels, as if it's their own fault, as if they somehow brought it on themselves. I know the shame of being "marked" somehow, of feeling I'd never fit in with others and the fear that they would find out my dirty secret. I know the sadness that comes from wanting all of this to go away and knowing nothing will ever be the same. Nothing will ever look, smell or feel normal again. Most of all, I know that anger you feel deep inside but can't share with anyone and can't seem to get rid of, no matter how hard you kick, scream and cry. And because I know this pain, I can relate to others, put myself in their shoes and help them through it. What I will never do is tell them to "get over it," "move on from that experience already," or "let it go." For that may be the worst pain of all. Instead I listen without judgment; I let them know that it's not their fault. That they had no control over this, none at all and nothing they could have done could have changed it.

What an amazing gift – to be able to talk to that hurting child - or adult with a hurting child inside – and help them finally tell the story that has been eating them up. I think back to my experience and I know without a doubt that this would never be possible had I not gone through it myself.

We all experience things differently and we would all change things in our past if we could. Now that I have children, I would do anything to protect them, and I certainly would not wish what I went through on anyone. And yet, at the same time I can say I would not change a thing. I have gained the ability to speak openly to anyone about this subject, and I recognize that in doing so I am part of a dramatic change needed for healing. I don't worry about making them uncomfortable, because I know that one day even that will change. I have gained the knowledge of what my body can do to protect itself and how far it will go – and I share that knowledge with others. Most importantly, I let other victims know they are not alone, that there is a way out of the darkness. And for this amazing gift, I am truly grateful.

YANINA RAMIREZ is an author, healer and a spiritual mentor who works with individuals to help them connect with the powers they have inside. In her intuitive counseling sessions, Yanina assists her clients in moving through past and present traumas and challenges, thus freeing them from victim mode and facilitating their journey to find their purpose.

Yanina resides in Glendale, Arizona with her son and two daughters. To find out more about her work or schedule a session, send her an email.

Connect with Yanina
yaninaramirez@mail.com

I am grateful for ...

Week 29

Today I choose to live with gratitude

for the love that fills my heart, the peace that

rests within my spirit, and the voice of hope

that says all things are possible.

~ Anonymous

ANSWERED PRAYER

They say dog people have one "Soul Dog" who comes into their lives. We love ALL of our special fur babies, of course, but the Soul Dog is the one we have such an intense and personal bond with that our communication and emotional attachment to them is on a whole different level.

Humphrey was my Soul Dog, and the reasons I was so bonded with him go way deeper than just your typical dog-owner relationship.

When I was twenty-seven years old, I became pregnant. This was an unprecedented event since I never thought I would physically be able to have children. The doctors had warned me after an invasive surgery that my endometriosis had been so severe that pregnancy was unlikely. I was excited for the miracle of a little one growing inside me. And then one day, sadly and suddenly, I lost my baby, and he was never to see the world. I tried to stay positive, but I felt as though a part of me had died ... which it had.

I couldn't get over losing my Richard. I cried just about every night, and I mourned the baby whom I would never see, or touch, or tell "I love you." I thought about him all the time, day and night. I couldn't let go. My son would never know the love of his mother, and it tore up my soul so badly that I sometimes couldn't breathe.

And then Mother's Day came, and I was lying in bed thinking how I wasn't a mother. Thinking that my baby was gone. Thinking that maybe it was something I did that made him go away. Thinking that I was such a horrible mama that I couldn't even protect my own child enough to even be able to bring him into the world.

As all of these thoughts swirled through my mind, and the hurt became unbearable, I cried out, "God, I can't take this anymore. I can't deal with it. The pain isn't going away! Please help me! Please."

A couple of days later, I went into work at the veterinary clinic where I was employed. Midway through the afternoon, one of the technicians came into the back room holding a small black furry animal. It appeared to be a gerbil from what I could see, but our veterinarian took charge of the fuzzy handful and loudly declared it was a newborn puppy and someone needed to take it home. I jumped at the chance while everyone else backed away; I was the only one delighted about such a sleep-deprived prospect.

The doctor examined the tiny ball of soft black fluff and told me, "You are going to have to take really good care of him. Bottle-feed him every four hours and watch him constantly. He's going to be like having a baby, okay?" She handed the warm bundle to me, having no idea of the impact of her next words. "He's your baby now. He was born three days ago, which means he was born on Mother's Day."

That meant the puppy had come into this world on the day I had sent up my plea. In that moment, I knew God had answered my prayer.

Every four hours, I bottle fed little Humphrey, cradling his tiny, half-pound body in my palm. By the time he was a month old, he weighed five pounds - five pounds of fluffy love who slowly was healing my heart. I no longer had the deep sorrow I'd been carrying around. It seemed God saw fit to send an angel to me in the form of a dog. And as the years went by, that furry bit of love saw me through everything - many moves, a divorce, a lay-off, a bankruptcy, a broken heart, a tragic death - and he also was there for all of my good times, too, like finding love and peace and happiness again.

After twelve wonderful years together, Humphrey was diagnosed with kidney failure and I was told I had only a short time left with him. I cried into his fur and told him over and over I wasn't ready for him to leave, that I still needed him in my life. My husband and I began at-home dialysis twice a day, and when Humphrey stopped eating, I syringe fed him Ensure and baby food every morning and every evening. It occurred to me, while I was sitting on the floor feeding him like a baby, that he and I had come full circle. As I looked into his milky, cataract-filled eyes, I realized that I was keeping him alive at the end just as I had at the beginning, and that he would always be my baby boy.

The day eventually came when I had to make the difficult decision - that inevitable, loving choice of setting my beloved dog free from pain. Letting Humphrey go was one of the most heart-wrenching moments of my life. He passed away peacefully in my arms while I whispered in his ear over and over, "I love you. I love you so much."

The impact Humphrey had on my life was so special, and I think anyone who has a Soul Dog understands my journey. Humphrey healed me when I needed it most, and he was a gift beyond measure. Gratitude doesn't adequately describe the joy and thankfulness I feel when I think of my fuzzy baby boy. And I know, in my heart of hearts, he and Richard are together in heaven; two guardian angels happily watching over their mama.

Namaste, my friends, and much love.

CHELLY BOSWORTH is a fictional romance novelist who adores daydreaming on paper. She uses her writing to give her readers a sense of community, a feeling of belonging and an escape from the stresses and pressures of everyday life.

A fiendish blogger, coffee lover and bookaholic, Chelly resides in Phoenix, Arizona with her husband and their two rescue dogs, The Murf and Larry Marie.

Connect with Chelly
chellybosworth.com

I am grateful for ...

Week 30

The struggle ends when gratitude begins.

~ Neale Donald Walsch

LIVING GRATEFULLY: SPANNING THE BRIDGE BETWEEN FEAR AND LOVE

It's relatively easy to feel gratitude when life's circumstances are flowing smoothly. But what happens when you are amid loss, crisis, devastation and mounting challenges? Is there any room in your life for gratitude when catastrophe hits? I used to think not. Now, I know differently. Now, I understand that gratitude is the magical bridge between fear and love.

Gratitude is the missing ingredient that dissolves all resistance. Gratitude opens your eyes to the majesty of creation. Is it always easy to walk across that bridge? Is it simple to embark upon a consistent practice of gratitude? Not necessarily. But is it worth it to develop such a practice? In my view, yes! However, I didn't easily come to that conclusion.

On November 22nd, 1994, my life imploded. I sat across from a well-respected psychologist who uttered a grim pronouncement that thrust me into an unimaginable vortex of pain. "Your son, Mark, has autism." Once the word autism was uttered, the life that I had known was inextricably over. I sat in complete shock trying to absorb one simple fact … my adorable, tow-headed, 21-month-old son, had autism. I wished I could escape from the implications of that dismal prognosis and instead revisit a past day of bliss - a day when gratitude flooded every fiber of my being. On that day of euphoria, I gazed into Mark's newborn eyes and held him in my arms for the first time. That moment came about because his birth mother graciously allowed me to become his adoptive Mom. Is there any gift potentially greater than the gift of life? In my view, there was no greater blessing than to be given the privilege of motherhood. Nevertheless, once autism shattered my belief in a fair, orderly, and sensible, world, that day of grace felt interminably far behind me. In my then-current yoke of numbness, I questioned whether I would ever experience another moment of peace, joy, exhilaration or gratitude again.

Inside, I carried a deep, abiding, longing for Mark to know me; to look in to my eyes; to say Mom, as he threw his arms around my neck; to sit by my side, while I read to him; to seek my comfort; to belly laugh in my presence; and to ask me why the stars burn brightly in the night sky. Once autism invaded, I carried grave doubts as to whether any of those bonds were possible. My biggest terror was whether Mark would move through his entire life unable to receive love or give love to others. My most catastrophic fear was that Mark would be expendable, languishing away in a facility for the forgotten. To assuage those fears, my ego convinced me that exerting my considerable will power toward recovering my son was the solitary solution. Therefore, I ran fast and furiously ahead with my plan.

At the onset of his therapy, I didn't realize the paradox confronting me; the grief process and the practice of gratitude could actually co-exist simultaneously. For years on end, as I watched my son putting maximum effort into mastering every isolated, minute, developmental milestone that most of us take for granted, my awareness of the preciousness of every single human capacity was exponentially heightened. However, during the six years that I was at the helm of Mark's early intervention program, I neglected to fully maximize that lesson. I momentarily celebrated his first wave, his first word and his first spontaneous imitation - but I didn't slow down enough to fully bask in the energy of gratitude. I was like a passenger aboard a high-speed train, heading toward an undisclosed destination with little to no time to take in the passing scenery. I lurched from crisis to crisis and became habituated to doing so. I was so immersed in achieving outcomes that I often missed the miracles that were right in front of me. Surprisingly, you can easily miss your own life, if you aren't present to it. My experiences taught me that it's the small, fleeting, personal moments of intimacy and connection that hold the most significance in life. No matter the weight of your circumstances, there is always room to savor the awe-inspiring nature of your personal encounters.

Learning to stay open as you more deeply enter life, fully present in your body and mindfully aware of your inner and outer realities, is a precursor to receiving life's blessings. Learning to fine-tune your observational powers will help you to appreciate the immeasurable number of blessings already present in your life. At the same time, it's vital that you also direct your point of focus back upon yourself. I completely lost sight of that principle because I was so intent on powering through my obsessive quest to make Mark indistinguishable from his typical peers. Eventually, I saw the benefits of shining the spotlight back upon myself. Life will invariably mirror back your alignment with honoring, appreciating and valuing yourself. When creating your daily gratitude tally, consciously make note and write down at least three gifts, remembering to consider how you can include yourself on your list. Ask yourself: What do I appreciate about myself? What are my unique qualities, gifts, contributions and talents? What efforts, big and small, have I made that elevate those around me?

Over time, I saw the value of looking at life through the lens of appreciation, and, as I did so, more magical circumstances to appreciate manifested before me. I saw firsthand the transformative power of offering thankfulness in advance of blessings that I envisioned and believed were already on their way to me. I gradually changed the tone of my conversations from blame, whine and complain to acknowledge, bless and appreciate. My health improved, my outlook transformed, my passion for life reignited, and my relationship with my son healed in a myriad of unexpected ways. Importantly, I recognized that energy spent yearning for outcomes that are not part of the overarching Divine plan will further delay and deny the superabundance of the universe.

Mark is twenty-five years old now. I now view him as my greatest teacher. Parenting is the place where you meet all parts of yourself in the mirror. My relationship with Mark has facilitated a deep dive into a rich and fulfilling healing experience that has allowed me to stretch myself further than I could ever have imagined. These experiences have facilitated a profound search for meaning in the midst of adversity and an unbounded appreciation for the untold number of hidden treasures buried within myself and at various locales along my journey.

A milder form of autism continues to impact Mark's daily life. During my early years speeding along that monorail, I could never have envisioned the distances I've now traveled or the large numbers of wonderful people along the route who have generously shaped my son for the better. Even more astounding is the way in which my travels have shaped me for the better. I feel unbridled gratitude for wisdom that I have gained, as I look at life through the expanded vista of thankfulness.

I could never have anticipated that I would become a more empowered, more authentically self-sufficient and courageous woman, as compared to the 38-year-old who sat in that psychologist's office, ironically, two days before the Thanksgiving holiday, back in 1994. I now see that it wasn't autism, per se, that stood in the way of me learning to appreciate the life I had been gifted. In truth, it was my resistance to it that kept me from fully embodying gratitude. In the end, it was everything that came along with autism that served, and continues to serve, as the catalyst for almost everything I know about recognizing and appreciating the infinite, seemingly-invisible sacred hand present in all aspects of life. Imagine – through gratitude my oppressive fears transformed into my greatest assets! What could be grander than that?

KAREN HASSELO is a Certified Spiritual Life Coach, is the Founder of Spirit First Coaching and a contributing author to No Mistakes: How You Can Change Adversity into Abundance, 2013 and When Heaven Touches Earth: A Little Book of Miracles, Marvels & Wonders, 2016.

After Karen's son was diagnosed with autism in 1994, she experienced the "dark night of the soul," which propelled her to master psycho-spiritual healing methods. Her mission is to help special needs mothers convert struggle into acceptance, inner peace, intuitive knowing and grace. Karen spent sixteen years as a clinical social worker who specialized with adolescents.

She received her M.A. in Social Work from The University of Chicago and is a graduate of the Holistic Learning Centers in New Jersey.

Connect with Karen
spiritfirstcoaching.com
Facebook.com @ SpiritFirstCoaching

I am grateful for ...

Week 31

What if you woke up tomorrow with

only the things you thanked God for today?

~ Unknown

EMBODY GRATITUDE

I remember when I first heard this question. I was at the end of my 200-hour yoga teacher training program, and the founder of the school came in to talk with our class. A group of 30 of us were listening to her talk about yoga, mindfulness, and gratitude. I don't recall the specific conversation leading up to this question. I think I was probably wandering in my mind, and when she asked us this question, I felt myself snap back into present moment. An eerie silence overcame the classroom.

I recall feeling a sinking in my stomach and a swelling in my heart. What if I only wake up tomorrow with the things I thanked God for today? Crap! I immediately started internally rattling off all the things I was thankful for: My kids, my husband, my home, my car, my job, my pets, my family, my friends ... I even went so far as to say thank you for my pen to write with and paper to write on. I was in full-on gratitude list mode; however, I did not actually feel grateful.

I felt afraid. I felt fear of those things not being present in my life. I felt ungrateful and even a little ashamed that I had not expressed gratitude for all the blessings in my life.

My heart caved in and my back rounded at the feeling of recognizing that I was definitely not taking time to be grateful and appreciative of all the love in my life. Although I didn't know it at the time, I was actually living in fear of losing everything.

I feel this is a very common misunderstanding among people who engage in gratitude practice. Oftentimes, when someone decides to start a gratitude list or a daily gratitude practice, they simply get a journal and start writing a list of five things a day they are grateful for. While this is a starting place, it can feel like a chore and that is not the true purpose of the practice.

I did this too. That night, I started a gratitude practice. I was diligent about writing each night in my journal a list of five things from that day that I was thankful for. Meanwhile, I continued rattling off that internal list of everything I couldn't stand to lose because I did not want God to take away anything that I love.

While I would go to sleep feeling a little lighter, I would still have an unsettled feeling in my stomach and heart.

It took me a little while to figure out what this was about. I began to realize that although I was writing gratitude, I was feeling frustration and fear. I was using this daily practice that was supposed to uplift me and bring forth more appreciation to actually reaffirm the already-present fear and sadness within my heart.

After this realization, I decided to learn how to do a gratitude practice the right way. Now, it may seem strange to think there is a right way, but after learning what I did, I do believe there is a right way to do this.

Here is what I started to do: I made a list of all the things throughout the day that made me smile. Instead of writing out gratitude, I started writing out the things that brought me happiness. This was a life-changer. Instead of focusing my energy on being grateful for what I feared losing, I began focusing my energy on what was present in my life that increased my happiness.

My gratitude practice at the end of each night became a time for reexperiencing that happiness. I knew I was onto something. I was no longer going to bed with that fearful feeling in my stomach and heart. Instead, I was falling asleep feeling peaceful, calm, and happy. I started to notice that happiness felt subtly warm, peaceful, and sweet inside my stomach and heart. I felt a softening and opening. Tension melted away, my shoulders relaxed, my mouth smiled. I had a moment of realization: "Hmmm...maybe it is more about the feeling of gratitude than the mental list."

I continued this exploration with curiosity. As I went through my days, I noted when I would feel that happiness, and ask my body and mind to make a mental marker of the moment and feeling. When I went to write each night, I recalled those moments—gratitude moments. As I wrote, instead of just writing out an arbitrary list of what I was grateful for, I paused, closed my eyes, and recalled in my body and mind the moments from that day. The feelings returned immediately, and when I wrote I found myself not only writing about the experience, but I was also writing about how it felt to feel that experience.

That is where the magic of gratitude started to shift things in my life. As I rested in the feeling of being grateful, I felt the energy grow and expand. I realized that during all those years of writing gratitude lists, I was only operating out of fear-based anxiety that something bad would happen. I was not in energetic congruence with gratitude. I was in fear writing about being thankful. That doesn't make sense, and since the world responds to energy, I was actually putting out, and then receiving, more fear.

I started embodying gratitude by employing the yogic practice of shifting from thinking and doing (mental lists and writing) to feeling and being (recalling the memory and sensing its energy in my body). As I practiced this teaching, I was able to come into congruence, and create from a space of pure appreciation for all the beauty in my life.

Each day I was noticing more moments of happiness, peace, and joy. Each day I was feeling more alive, joyful, and excited for life. The more I chose to feel the moment and mentally label it as happiness, the more my energy started living in that state. I created an internal revenue bank of happiness moments that I could pull from at any time.

My invitation to you is this: Come into energetic alignment with gratitude. Release the gratitude list based on fear and instead embody the felt sense of gratitude by pausing to feel it and be in it. Take time each day to slow down and feel the moment of happiness. Note how that shows up in your body. Ask your body and mind to make a marker of that moment. If the feeling of true gratitude is new to you, let that be okay. It may feel uncomfortable at first to experience this pure feeling of happiness and joy. If you are used to living in fear, it may take some time to develop the capacity to feel great joy. Trust that in time, as you practice, it will feel more accessible to stay in this feeling for longer periods of time.

At the end of each day, reflect on these moments of gratitude. Recall the feeling of them in your body. Write about that. Write about what it felt like to feel happy, to be in a state of gratitude. Day by day, you will build your memory bank of happiness, and deplete the fear. Over time, your life will shift to align with more beauty and love, as you are resting in the energy of gratitude.

KATE SHIPP is a certified Yoga Therapist, Reiki Master Teacher, and Intuitive Coach. She empowers you to cultivate safety within your body and guides you to embrace your shadows by removing the veils of shame darkening your light. She takes you on a journey to reconnect with and nurture the inner child waiting for your love and affection.

Kate facilitates from a place of integrity and immovable faith that comes from her own fearlessness in healing and integrating past traumas to reveal a joy-filled, abundantly blessed life. She holds a safe, compassionate space for you to remember your wholeness, to see yourself from the lens of worthiness and grace, to embody your birthrights of peace and joy, and to fully thrive!

Kate resides in Peoria, AZ with her husband, two children, and 2 fur-babies. She sees private clients in-person and virtually.

Connect with Kate
kateshippyoga.com
Instagram @kateshipp333
Facebook.com @ thewindowwithin

I am grateful for ...

Week 32

Whatever we are waiting for - peace of mind, contentment,

grace, the inner awareness of simple abundance- it will surely

come to us, but only when we are ready to receive it

with an open and grateful heart.

~ Sarah Ban Breathnach

WITH EYES OF COMPASSION

My hand pulled the door shut ever so gently so as not to jar my racing heart and those of my three children inside. Oh, how I hated to close the door! The rush of movement to get out of the house on time, the list of items running through my head in a rhythmic chant; soccer uniform … check; package to be mailed … check; lunches packed - wait - where's my cell phone? My arms held a carefully stacked pile in perfect balance, yet I felt anything but steady. It was another weekday morning, accompanied by that nagging feeling of not doing enough to get my three daughters off to a perfect start. My perspiring forehead and racing heart made sitting back into the seat of the car unnatural. Yet, as I maneuvered out of the garage my head managed to calculate just how many minutes were left to arrive at work on time and it quickly concluded that I had left too late. Again.

How many times could this overwhelming burst of pressure rush through my chest? I never knew a body could produce that awful sensation so often in a given day. Forgetting to sign the papers from school, back-to-back meetings all day, and a lack of meaningful connection with my husband had caused me to feel like I was drowning. What mother isn't, I rationalized, telling myself that this was just "the way it was." I wondered if this was perhaps a badge of honor I wore to prove I was enough, as if busyness were a surefire way to achieve the "she's a great mom" recognition I desired.

My after-work day typically looked and felt the same. There were little people waiting for me to take them to practice, to pick them up from afterschool activities, to make a dinner that filled their hungry stomachs. But today, as autopilot-rushing mode took over, a persistent voice assertively declared, "There HAS to be something more to life than this." In all of my default reactions to the chaos, it never occurred to me that it could be different. Looking straight ahead, I blinked, as if my eyes were adjusting to a very bright spotlight that had suddenly been flipped on, illuminating the darkness of my panic. It was this inner knowing that affirmed that I could regain the sense of inner peace my soul desperately longed for. It did not matter that I had fed my head a daily dose of unrealistic expectations, poor boundaries and failure to speak up for my needs. Yes, something within me was stirring. I could not possibly comprehend in that moment the freedom of being less defined by what I do and more defined by who I am.

That night seemed the same as any other; I was barely able to keep my eyes open long enough to put the girls to bed. And, like most nights, sleep came immediately and ended far too quickly. It was some time around five in the morning that I woke to the light shining under the closed bathroom door. The morning routine was beginning again, but I had twenty precious more minutes before I had to get out of bed, so I drifted off again. In this short period of time I was taken to a familiar lakeshore and listening to the sound of my children's uncontrolled laughter as they were chased around a yard lined with enormous shade trees. I watched the action with this feeling of joy and exhilaration, as if I was running right alongside them. Just out of my view, I could see someone was approaching. Standing about ten feet away, his white fisherman's hat, silver-framed glasses and red and blue striped rugby made an impression and his smile was instantly recognizable. Dad! He was here! Holding out his hand to me, I thrust my own hand towards his and just as we were about to touch, I woke up. Lying frozen in bed I heard my dad's loving voice say so clearly, "You are so deserving." His departed soul was delivering a message and a rush of energy came over me and filled my heart with compassion. It had been easy for me to see when someone else needed a pass or a gentle nod to let him or her know that mistakes happen. Now I was being reminded that I was worthy of the same care and consideration. The tender message pivoted me so significantly that I discovered a soulful place of power to see myself from a new perspective.

My self-care journey was beginning and despite a desire to make dramatic changes overnight, it was the small shifts with plenty of trial and error that helped me gain more appreciation, self-acceptance and resilience. Little practices began to quiet my fear voice, awaken my internal sense of calm and help me trust myself more. These days, outside chaos no longer drives my life or defines my emotions; instead, I start from within as the source of my true power. Listening to my heart defines what I do and how I respond. Let your heart be your guide. It is the GPS back to your soul.

- ♥ Begin with moments of mindfulness – These are small glimpses throughout the day that make you smile such as watching a toddler playing, hearing a favorite song or smelling a delightful scent. These moments shift your energy and bring awareness to the now. There is nothing too small to appreciate.

- ♥ Be present with your heart – When the mind races with thoughts, this action provides relief: place your hands over your heart and breathe in. Count to four, then slowly breathe out. Repeat. Bringing your presence into your heart space connects you to what is true.

- ♥ Mind your thoughts – Judging others spreads drama and creates negative energy. You can never know for sure what motivates other people, but you can learn what you are accepting or judging in yourself.

- ♥ Feel your feels – Emotions that are pushed down become bigger. Allow strong and difficult feelings space to rise and pass naturally. You may very well find something great waiting for you on the other side.

- ♥ Trust yourself – We all make mistakes. By letting go of the past you can allow what you've learned to become your strength.

Most importantly, look in the mirror with eyes of compassion. Your life is precious, and my purpose is to remind you that YOU are so deserving!

KAREN COWPERTHWAITE (aka "Souly Sister") is a Life Coach and Intuitive Guide for women who are ready to create a more soul-satisfying life for themselves. With loving support guided by the wisdom of the angels and Spirit, Karen's gentle, intuitive life coaching provides a sacred, highly individualized process that allows clients to discover the purpose of their struggles, gain insight into their experiences, and shift their thoughts and behaviors from "auto pilot" to a new empowered perspective. Karen is also a co-author of Amazon Best Sellers 365 Days of Angel Prayers and 111 Morning Meditations.

Connect with Karen to schedule a complimentary discovery session to connect with your soul's purpose and Download her free audio meditation Renew Your Heart Empower Your Soul.

Connect with Karen
soulysister.com
karen@soulysister.com

I am grateful for ...

Week 33

Train yourself never to put off the word or

action for the expression of gratitude.

~ Albert Schweitzer

GRATITUDE IS A CHOICE

The Universe works in mysterious ways, and it proves itself over and over again. When this project came across my desk, I felt immediately repulsed. "What the heck do I have to be grateful for?" I asked myself poignantly when reading what the subject was and instantaneously moved to a state of confusion. Gratitude is something that was inherent in me because it was almost forced. Being brought up a good Catholic Italian girl, we were taught from the moment we could comprehend that gratitude is par for the course. You give thanks for everything. I tried throughout my life to maintain an attitude of gratitude, but there are some times where it's harder than others.

The end of last year was tumultuous at best for me. My personal, business and financial life was in shambles, yet I tried to hold my head up high and take it in stride. To see the lessons within the suffering because plain and simple, it felt like suffering. I felt lost. While embroiled within my personal turmoil I decided to reframe and restructure by taking a hold of my life and set the intentions for the best year to come. It was New Year's Eve, and I decided instead of revelry, fireworks, and alcohol I was going to attend a New Age New Year Eve intentional session. We spent time learning about nature and taking in what the world has to offer. It was an interesting experience, however, what I took away from it was intention is 90% of the battle.

I wrote my intentions out to make them a tangible thing. A physical 'something' I could look upon and manifest into my reality. In my mind, once I wrote them out, they existed. They became something I could see touch and feel. They were a part of my reality starting from that moment, and all I needed to do was manifest my desires. What I learned from this exercise was that I was constantly being led back to gratitude. I try, but I'm only human. I focus on what I want, not what I have. Every time I got so wrapped up in the need or desire my spirit brought me back to gratitude. It was confusing, to say the least.

So here I sit, sharing my lesson on gratitude and its one that I am still in the process of learning. Being grateful is easy when life is good- it comes naturally and effortlessly. In good times, gratitude allows us to magnify and celebrate the goodness. However, when life goes badly, giving thanks is not so simple. In fact, it can be downright agonizing; no one feels grateful when they lose a job, a friend or even their health. In time the lesson in this for me became quite clear- there is a distinct difference in FEELING grateful and BEING grateful.

When I break it down, I have to go to the basics. I am eternally grateful I am still among the living ... to have the ability to learn. There are so many who were denied that right. I have had many negative things happen to me- for example, I came close to death on several occasions. In the recent past, I endured what could only be called a botched surgery. A surgeon made a mistake that almost cost me my life. Due to that mistake, infection ravaged my body, and I lost my uterus, part of my small intestines and had to have my stomach wall rebuilt. I was devastated as I felt part of myself was ripped away without my consent. I felt that my health and more importantly my femininity was taken from me. It was in the months of weakness, in recovery that I found my strength. It was during those times when I felt all was lost that I found my faith. It was then that I realized how fleeting life could be. It was then that I began my journey to wholeness through learning about the mind, body, spirit connection.

That experience propelled me into a new life path that encompassed everything I knew I could be. While in my three-month recovery I started studying the connection. It's the perfect trinity of connectedness. When they all work together life is great, so I studied everything in my power to facilitate my recuperation. I read everything I could get my hands on, and when I was whole, I was ready to conquer the world. It was through that awful, life altering experience that I could become more joyful in the situations presented to me thereafter, and more determined to succeed.

I can absolutely BE grateful in these moments, but can I feel it? I can honestly say I didn't feel it right away. I adapted the 'fake it until you make it' attitude and plugged along. Willing oneself to be grateful, therefore less depressed or less sad in the hard times is no easy task as we don't have total control of our emotions but what CAN we do? What we can do is choose. We can choose to be grateful because gratitude is a choice. Gratitude provides a perspective from which we can view life in its totality and not be overwhelmed by whatever temporary circumstances life has thrown at us. I made a conscious choice to be grateful for the experience. I gave thanks for everything around me from the medicines that helped heal me to the smiles of my children that cheered me up. Every little thing became a lesson in gratitude and gratefulness.

Life CAN suck. In fact, there are still periods where I question every lesson I've ever learned because it seemed the universe was dumping all its useless crap on me without provocation. I felt as if I was on a roller coaster of events that spent more times in the valleys than in the hills. I spent time trying to overcome sorrow, clawing myself out of self-destruct mode all while literally dying inside. It's in those low moments, those valleys if you will, that I have learned through gratitude to stop, reframe and choose.

What do I have to be grateful for in this moment?

It took a long time for me to be able to stop and think of gratitude in my lowest moments but it's there. I started small and took it step-by-step, moment-by-moment. I was grateful for my pulse, my senses, the air, etc. and I would branch out. I then saw and felt everything I am grateful for and was able to break out of my deepest funks. It has become a part of the lesson now to say I am grateful for every single negative thing that has ever happened to me for I believe that these trials from the universe have always brought me a life lesson. Some are incredibly profound – very much like this awareness itself. It is that from the darkest of times that I have learned to truly be grateful for the light. Choosing to be grateful and feeling grateful became the focus of my intentions.

Once I shifted my thoughts to becoming grateful, and in essence embracing and embodying gratitude, things began to change. Small inklings of what I wanted to manifest started to appear, and I was acutely aware. Gratitude started to come easily in each awareness. The trickles came in bursts of recognition … some subtle and some blinding. I asked for guidance, I asked to be surrounded by those who loved and recognized me, and I asked for harmony. I asked for a sense of peace when I didn't even realize I needed it. I asked to be allowed to see myself as who I really was again … I hadn't even realized I had lost sight of it. I asked for the smile I had lost. I asked for permission to honor and acknowledge the light in myself that I had become blinded to. That same light that had been trampled. I asked for the ability for me to be myself without judgment. I asked just to be me again.

I now look at the piece of paper where I wrote out what I wanted. This palpable, solid entity that held what I needed at that moment almost a year ago and I am instantly transported back to that instant of desolation and need. I can still feel the pain and depths of my anguish as I recall forcing myself out of that space to reframe the pain into aspiration. I wrote about the peace and strength I required and even the type of people I needed to attract in my life down to the tiniest detail. It became my own little vision board as I started to see in my mind's eye what my life was going to become. The words on that paper gave me hope and something to physically look at and touch when I needed to be reminded what all this was for. I held on to that. I made the choice to move forward when all I wanted to do was to give up and give in. I chose to see the goodness in the experiences the Divine had bestowed upon me, and I chose to be grateful for them. I found that the worst things in life brought out the best in me.

Trials and suffering seemed to be refining and deepening my gratitude. I rewrote the soundtrack in my head from victim mode to victor, seeing each stride as another step towards peace. I was beginning to become grateful for every little aspect. During times of uncertainty, I realized how powerless I was to control my own destiny. Sure, we all have free will, but the truth is, there were many things that I was powerless over. The weather, the actions of others, gravity, traffic. I couldn't control every aspect of my life; at most, I could merely contribute and not all that much. That awareness in itself was hard enough to accept, but it did help me see things easier. By focusing on my behavior, my attitude, and my choices, I was able to control the few things that made all the difference to me and those around me. It helped me let go of some of the guilt surrounding my circumstances. I was able to see quite clearly that everything I had and everything I counted on could be taken away in an instant, which made it difficult for me to take those things for granted. And in that, I reclaimed my power with gratitude.

Processing life experiences with a grateful frame of mind does not mean denying negativity. Instead, it means realizing the power you have to change a problem into a prospect. It means relabeling a hurt into a potential advantage, altering negativity into positive frequencies for gratitude. Be Grateful before you feel grateful, for thoughts create feelings- Gratitude is a Choice!

I am grateful for the conflict, for within the conflict I find my strength. It is within my deepest depressions that the beauty of my strength shines through. Just like a diamond is forged from the strongest pressure or a pearl formed from an injured oyster we can choose to see the injury, or we can choose to see the results. We can choose to wallow in self-pity or be grateful for the awareness and lessons to be learned. I choose to not only see but to BE the brilliance among the strife. I choose to not only see but also be the rose among the thorns because it is those thorns that make me appreciate the divine splendor of the roses that much more.

VICTORIA LORELLI-LESSELL ACT, CHt, CLC is an Advanced Cupping Therapist, Clinical Hypnotherapist, Certified Life Coach, Energy Worker/Healer, Spiritual Teacher, Certified Mind Body Spirit Practitioner, Reiki and Munay–Ki Master.

Through her gifts, ability and unconditionally loving spirit she is able to connect with you and your authentic self on many levels. In her youth, she was a freelance writer and owned her own successful production company that collaborated with a variety of companies in the New York City area.

In 2007, Victoria changed her life path. She spent several years raising her family all while seeking her true passion in life- energy work. She began to slowly hone her natural skills by studying and graduating with honors from the prestigious Southwest Institute of the Healing Arts and becoming certified through the International Cupping Therapy Association solidifying her expertise. She now owns her own Holistic practice at 8400 South Kyrene Road Suite 127, Tempe, AZ 85284.

Connect with Victoria
SolenneHolistics.com
victoria.solenne@gmail.com
Facebook @ solenneholistic
480.206.7516

I am grateful for ...

Week 34

Being thankful is not always experienced as a

natural state of existence, we must work at it, akin to

a type of strength training for the heart.

~ Larissa Gomez

FINDING GRATITUDE IN THE RAIN

Gratitude. I choose to walk through my life in gratitude. It is a practice which I have embraced for many years and which has transformed my life. I have experienced so much more peace, serenity and happiness in my life simply by adjusting my attitude to appreciate the present, the now. What a realization this is. What a gift it is to experience. I have learned that one can be grateful when wonderful things are happening in one's life and when challenging experiences show up in one's life. And the latter, the challenging experience, certainly showed up for my husband and I this past year.

Who could say that one could be or would be grateful for a serious health diagnosis? No one wants to be sick or found to have a life-threatening illness. However, it happened that I found gratitude within the scariest time of my life. On December 12, 2017, my husband of 41 years was diagnosed with a Stage 4 Laryngeal Cancer. We both took this information hard. It was so frightening. How could this be? A wave of fear came over me. I was in disbelief. I so was shocked I wasn't able to sleep. And I wasn't able to eat much either.

I found myself in a puddle of tears and worry. It was only in the middle of the night, that I sought God to help me through. It was by this turning to God, Source of all Life, and Spirit that I found the strength and courage to face this challenge. Each day I asked for the strength to get through it all. With strength and courage, gratitude showed up. As that happened, I moved into a very present moment experience. I found that by staying in the present moment, I was able to get to the next moment. If I stepped out of the present moment, I found myself in fear once more, worries overwhelming me. So, moment by moment I walked.

I moved quickly to research the condition. I read everything I could find on success stories of others who had faced a stage 4 diagnosis. I read about natural treatments, Chinese Traditional Medicine, herbal therapy, the Budwig Protocol. I read about how to combine natural therapies successfully with conventional treatment. And I set about procuring these natural foods to support the process my husband was about to begin.

It was not the Christmas I had planned. I found myself in the waiting room as my husband had surgery to keep his airway open. When the surgeon came out, he reported that he came through very well. I was grateful. Later while in the ICU unit as my husband's recovery continued, I was grateful for the skilled head nurse who was caring for my husband that evening. I continued to find gratitude throughout my husband's hospital stay. I was grateful for the kindness of the post-surgical team of nurses and for their skill in respiratory therapy. I was grateful for my husband's quick recovery from surgery and for all the health personnel who helped us. I found gratitude as healing began, and as treatments started. One morning at the oncology center, a woman came up to me and asked if she could pray for my husband and I. I was deeply moved and so grateful for this act of kindness and love. Another time at a doctor's appointment I found a well of gratitude when we learned that 70% of the tumor was resolved. Then later in the process when no sign of the tumor could be found, we were so very grateful.

Gratitude is a daily way of being. It can be if you choose it. If you do, you realize a greater appreciation for everything around you. Your senses expand and your sense of being shifts. You have a greater sense of wholeness, completeness, and depth of being. What I have learned through this experience is that gratitude does not depend on good or bad events happening. It is there for our taking should we choose to be within its expansiveness. Gratitude is a choice and when you tap into the goodness of it so much more is available to you. Harmony, calm, serenity, and joy are within it.

I am grateful for the blessings that have come during and through this health challenge. The greatest blessing is that my husband and I have a deeper love and appreciation for each other. We have a deeper appreciation for life itself. This is a great gift and it is my hope that others learn how to walk through their lives in gratitude for what is and what is becoming. We have been blessed in so many ways. We celebrated his early success by taking a trip to the shore and to a wildlife sanctuary so serene and peaceful. We celebrated continued success by attending our niece's wedding. It was a joy to be there with our family who had gathered for this special occasion. We have been blessed with new friendships and people who ask, "Hi, how are you doing?" We are both so grateful that he has been able to return to work at the college where he has taught for many years. We have been blessed that my work situation has been so flexible and the people so understanding. We have been blessed with an outpouring of love from family and friends. Yes, gratitude showed up for this walk in the rain. Moment to moment, breath by breath.

LINDSLEY SILAGI is an educator and professional coach with a private coaching practice, Step By Step Results!, located in Santa Teresa, New Mexico where she lives happily with her husband, Lon.

Lindsley loves dance, art, music, nature, little kids, hot springs, gardening, books, striking up a friendship, photography, and travel.

Connect with Lindsley
lindsley.silagi@gmail.com

I am grateful for ...

Week 35

The root of joy is gratefulness.

~ David Steindl-Rast

A BEDTIME RITUAL OF GRATITUDE

Many people have a hard time falling asleep at night. Their minds race with random thoughts or they may replay something that happened during the day. Many times, there is a focus on all of the unpleasant things that occurred during the day and we can often find ourselves filled with worry or anxiety of what may happen tomorrow.

Scientific studies have shown that as we fall asleep, we become more and more immersed in an imaginative and hallucinatory world, and it is the thoughts we think before falling asleep that can dictate the dreams (or nightmares) we will have. Knowing this, and knowing the power of gratitude, I believe it is imperative that we load up our mind with thoughts of gratitude as we are drifting off to sleep.

What can a gratitude ritual at bedtime do for us? I believe it raises our optimism and gives us a happier send-off to dreamland. It makes us aware of the good things in our lives and can help keep pessimism and worry at bay. Be honest with yourself; which type of thoughts would you prefer to fall asleep with – thoughts of worry or thoughts of positivity and happiness?

Before I adopted my nightly bedtime ritual of gratitude, my sleep quality was erratic. Some nights I would wake up frequently with a headache or from a weird dream. Other times I would sleep all night but wake up feeling a type of heaviness in my consciousness, a sure indicator that my brain had been focused on heavy thoughts while I slept.

I had read much about the benefits of a nightly gratitude practice and decided to give it a try. Many sources suggested setting aside time each night to make a list of five or more things you were grateful for that had occurred that day. I, however, knew two things I wanted in whatever practice I adopted; number one, I wanted to implant good thoughts directly into my brain and number two I wanted to do something that was closer to the actual point of falling asleep. Here is the ritual I now perform every night as I am falling asleep.

Lying in bed, I snuggle down into my favorite sleeping position. I then take three deep breaths and tell my mind that I am going to remember and "say" three things (sometimes more) I am grateful for on this day. I then say those things to myself and conjure up a picture and feeling to go along with each one. For example, hardly a night goes by that does not include my gratitude for my 22-month-old grandson. He brings such joy and fun to my life every day. The gratitude I offer and say in my mind might be, "I am grateful for the fun I had with Nathan today. That boy brings me such joy and I love the way I feel when our laughter fills the room." I then feel that joy, often smiling as I see a picture of Nathan playing with his cars or dancing to a favorite tune.

I don't restrict myself to offering gratitude only for things that occurred that day. I'll often offer gratitude in advance for something I wish to manifest. Or I will offer gratitude for a certain way I felt, as in, "I am grateful for the feeling of relief I felt when the dentist told me I did not need to have that painful tooth crowned."

I have been following this nightly ritual for several years and believe it is my gratitude practice which has improved my sleep. There are many nights when I don't even get through all of my gratitudes before I have drifted off. I usually wake in the morning feeling rested and calm, which I believe is directly attributable to planting good-feeling thoughts into my mind/brain the night before.

I encourage you to try this practice for at least thirty days in order to have it become a nightly ritual for you. You will be amazed at the results and grateful for each night of restful, peaceful sleep you receive.

SUSAN OPEKA is the founder and owner of The Present Moment, Inc. which is a hub for programs, practitioners and merchandise dedicated to providing inspiration and building community. As the founder of the One Thought Away project she encourages individuals to focus on their thoughts in order to feel better and offers support through her Facebook group of the same name along with merchandise for the project in her e-commerce store, UpliftingGoods.com.

Susan also leads women's business groups and is a business strategist who helps solopreneurs and private professionals focus on bringing clarity to the foundations in their business. She presents and teaches her self-developed organizational methodology – Eating the Elephant: One Bite at a Time – to groups of all sizes.
Be sure to visit her online specialty retail store at UpliftingGoods.com.

Connect with Susan
ThePresentMomentInc.com
sopeka@thepresentmomentinc.com

I am grateful for ...

Week 36

Gratitude will shift you to a higher frequency

and will attract much better things.

~ Rhonda Bryne

MY GRATEFUL JOURNEY

When Kim Richardson invited me to contribute to this book and what gratefulness meant to me, the answer was quick and absolute. I am so Grateful that my journey has started. I love being on my journey towards living mindfully, everything I'm learning, and healing my inner-child. You see, this journey to real happiness meant stopping. And restarting. I stopped living with all the finesse of a sledgehammer and finally realized true happiness must be somewhere deeply hidden inside myself. Thus, my journey to find it began.

It started with my second blended-family divorce, talk about crash and burn. I had again thought I was the most awesome stepmom ever and that all my adult step-kids would adore me, my new husband would protect me, we would easily solve any problems that arose and that we would all live forever happy as a loving "family." Wrong. Once again, there was a target on my forehead for sabotage and being picked-apart. Everything I did with loving intentions was for naught and nobody at any time adored me after I said, "I Do."

This is a good time to mention that false expectations may have been the culprit here. I had hit rock bottom and was totally shell-shocked from a 4th divorce and 2nd divorce from blended-family disaster. I received very little support then from anyone, due to poor relationships with my family. I had no idea why this had happened again, why they had turned on me, or what to do. I was filled with shame and had no idea who I was anymore. Failure is lonely companion.

Since I needed to move out of his house, I actually had the foresight to think about myself for once, and the fact that I LOVE water. Love being in it, sitting next to it and looking at it. Water calms me and is food for my soul. So, I held out for the pool view apartment I really wanted and moved into the guest room I had once designed for my stepdaughter. This was not a fun time but making even a small decision can turn out to be a pivotal first moment of our own journey, instead of living to make others happy. This is how I found myself at age 60 living alone for the first time in my life, in a rather cute apartment with a view of the prettiest pool. Much to my surprise, I began to love that apartment, the fitness center next to the pool, my nice neighbors and surprisingly, living alone. Everything in my apartment was exactly what and how, I wanted it. Hmmm, I was kind of happy maybe?

Around that time, I discovered podcasts purely by accident when I overheard a co-worker quietly listening to one while working. They sounded similar to talk-radio and were something new to my shallow-lived life. I began searching for more podcast topics of interest to me, as my mind gradually opened to learning new things and the strange idea of making myself happy instead of others. A whole new level of self-awareness and soul-searching emerged as I absorbed motivational and educational podcasts of different levels. Then, I then got a second job doing something I really enjoyed, rocked a personal budget, started an IRA and retirement planning and decided I was going to experience and live in all the places I'd ever desired!

This step of my journey is where I started embracing the possibility that I could actually make a pretty great life for myself, by myself and that I could be a better, happier and much more contented person while living more simply. The world of podcasts was a wonderful platform where I learned I wasn't alone in thinking I basically sucked at life and needed to make some very real and lasting changes. They lifted me, kept me company, motivated and educated me. I learned to love myself, which is the key to it all.

I admitted that I had to re-create myself and learn to appreciate the very few things that were right in my life. I made myself be grateful for my cute tiny apartment, my job and for being healthy enough to still work. I started making new friends, fixed up my tiny front porch with lots of flowers and hung a hummingbird feeder out my window I inherited a rescue dog, which allowed me to walk barefoot on the grass outside my apartment and appreciate the landscaping.

The relationships I had contributed to screwing up, I now addressed. Although I did a pitifully poor job of it, the important ones got better with time. Some relationships were not meant to be as I learned that part of healing the inner-child who haunts me, was making the decision to become the loving protector that sweet little girl who just wanted to be loved and wanted, never had. I learned that healing her is a huge part of the journey to my highest good.

While I wasn't even aware it was happening, I had adopted a steadfast gratefulness and filled my life with so much learning and light that there wasn't any room left for the pain. Two years later, my journey is soaring! I am still a work in progress, but through a lot of self-help work, I discovered a peace that only we can bring ourselves. I learned that there are always going to be more levels to happiness, but we have to already be grateful and happy in the level we're on and to be open, in order to advance even higher.

If you are going through a bad season of life, don't give up! We have unlimited resources available in book stores and free podcasts in the self-help arena. Be discerning of your choices but go take that first step. You CAN make your life better and begin to live in the spirit of gratefulness. You CAN learn to love yourself and live peacefully. You CAN make yourself happy and deserve it!

Let this book be the start of your journey to your highest self. Where do you want it to take you? Quiet your mind and meditate at the start of every day to whatever higher source you believe in. Visualize your best life, and most of all, create your days with your highest good as the goal.

The idea was already forming to write a book about being a successful Stepmom with adult kids, so one day I went to a book & author fair in the town where I live. Kim Richardson was one of the authors and I attended her interesting workshop. Strangely, this beautiful soul had already visited my life thru my reading a Sunny Dawn Johnston book, in which a period of Kim's life was featured. Kim is the kind of person that once she's entered your life, you'll never want her to leave it. I'm immensely in her debt for providing this opportunity to contribute to this awesome book!

I'm also grateful that part of my journey has been working on weight loss and eating healthy, which is what Kim is all about. She has inspired me, so I eat gluten-free as much as possible and have a garden in which I grow organic vegetables. I've also planted blackberries, blueberries and fruit trees. Your journey is like a tree, it has many wonderful branches!

Always researching motivational and interesting things, I came upon an event called Celebrate Your Life, which holds workshops and all things related to mind-body-spirit based living. Bingo! I was interested and attended. From there I found an Entrepreneur/Writer's Workshop. The cost was way out of my comfort zone but decided to take the risk since I had reached a new and intriguing level of investing in myself!

What I discovered in that workshop was that I have the very real ability to help others. I've made all the Stepmom mistakes and don't want you to, so I'm writing a book for those in Stepmom rolls who struggle. Maybe you care too much about the kids, or your partner isn't being supportive, or there's an ex sabotaging you. It can be hard! If you need to reach out to me, I am here. Try to feel the love being sent your way, you are not alone. The unique problems Stepmom's have to navigate can be challenging no matter what type of modern family you are a member of.

Now it is your turn to start your journey. Whatever changes you need to make, take the first step and be mindful of living your best life, every day. You're going to be so happy! I promise.

Let gratitude and loving yourself be your guide,

Sandra

SANDRA GRAY lives in Payson, Arizona with her husband Ken and their three dogs. She and her husband are avid Scuba Divers and frequently travel for their favorite sport. She has two daughters and two step-sons. Sandra no longer tries to control outcomes with step-kids. Sometimes things go great and sometimes not, but she has learned to remain peaceful anyway. She is enough.

It is Sandra's intention to get the book out and to lead workshops on what being a successful Stepmom entails. It is her purpose to create a community of people who will support each other.

Her book is being written and ORGANIC STEPMOM GROUP.com will soon be there for you. It will be a helpful resource for the unique problems stepmom's face and will be a mind-body-spirit approach to navigating and being the "outsider" successfully! Look for it in 2019!

Connect with Sandra
sandragray@organicstepmomgroup.com

I am grateful for ...

Week 37

Gratitude is the sweetest thing in a seekers life - in all human life. If there is gratitude in your heart, then there will be tremendous sweetness in your eyes.

~ Sri Chinmoy

GRATITUDE LESSONS FROM GRANDMOTHER'S FRONT PORCH SWING

My paternal grandmother, Agnes Littlejohn Clayton, was the matriarch of our family with deep spiritual faith and a heart of gold. My grandmother maintained a beautiful home with thriving vegetable and flower gardens in a small village of Maplewood, Ohio, where our dairy and crop farm was only a couple of miles away. During my 17 years of growing up on our farm, she faithfully would arrive in our kitchen daily offering a freshly baked pie or the latest news.

Each Sunday after church services, we never missed a home-cooked dinner in my grandmother's formal dining room, where she frequently served up mouth-watering, pan-fried chicken and her specialty sweet potato salad. Before each meal, we prayed and gave thanks for the food on her table, our health and well-being and for higher trust and faith that everything on our farm would be blessed in bountiful ways. "We must always give thanks first for what we do have before we ask for anything more," were grandmother's pre-prayer reminder words to us.

One Sunday summer day, after another delicious dinner, my grandmother and I had a rare opportunity to sit on her front porch swing. I was a very active teenager who was most interested in boys and being cool, so our time together was less frequent. Her front porch swing served as our social conversation time together. She would share her insights on life regarding current situations and with her keen listening skills, she could also uncover what was happening in my life.

On that day, I shared with grandmother what I considered to be hardships of teenage years living on a farm instead of living in town where kids were considered "cool" by having all the latest gadgets and fun gatherings. In response, she asked me what I was grateful for in my life that I considered cool.

My gratitude list included a transistor radio, my own room with a canopy bed, three new mini-skirts my great aunt Marjorie sewed that were identical to the department store models, and my new Timex watch.

My grandmother smiled and asked, "What about your intelligence, your loving heart, the way you care for children, the woods you love to explore, the sparkly rocks you collect, the four-leaf clovers you find frequently and the invitations you receive from town friends to visit their fun gatherings? What are you grateful for that makes you cool and doesn't cost money?"

At first, I was resistant in having grandmother divert what I really wanted or thought I needed as a teenager to be cool. She was very generous in slipping a few dollars in our pocket to purchase what we needed when it was necessary. Yet, my grandmother's greatest gifts were being a teacher by profession and spiritual leader of strong faith in our family, her community and village church. She had intuitive wisdom, words of higher guidance and life lessons to share in which many times I felt came from Angels.

When she gently yet firmly said, "Listen to me further please," I tuned in to her words as I knew something was about to shift in me. She continued by swinging a bit faster on her porch swing as her voice filled with passion. "Gratitude starts in your heart and is a feeling of appreciation for living life. It's not about things you acquire to be cool or fit in. You give thanks for those things if and when they arrive as they will make you feel good temporarily, but that good feeling of gratification wears off easily. Gratitude is different. Gratitude lives in your heart and is the direct communication line to God. When we give thanks in our prayers, we also need to feel and express deep gratitude for living a wonderful life, along with its challenges that God has given us. Gratitude is a living feeling inside of our hearts that makes us feel good ALL the time, not only when we acquire certain things. It is a lasting feeling."

I was definitely intrigued in knowing how to sustain this good feeling consistently, yet being true to my teenage know-it-all attitude, I retorted by saying I was indeed grateful and did say thank you often as I was a polite and obedient granddaughter. Grandmother's porch swing lesson continued, "Saying thank you is an action of gratitude that comes from your heart, not your head or what you think you should say by being polite. Your mind makes you think you need all these things in life to feel good, yet your heart possesses gratefulness for everything you are experiencing in life by feeling love and appreciation. Stay focused on the feeling of gratitude inside your heart as this is where true abundance happens. Gratitude multiplies all wonderful things in life and makes us rich without money. It also serves as a healing salve for our heart wounds when bad things happen. Eventually in time, you will always see the gift in deep grief of loss or a difficult lesson given and be grateful it came to you. Gratitude is the foundation law of loving life."

I've taken many philosophy and sociology classes in my undergraduate and graduate years of higher education, yet I never heard one professor who could explain gratitude and its benefits in my grandmother's way she relayed to me on that summer day. I wrote a paper for my graduate philosophy class regarding the benefits of gratitude as this living feeling inside my heart that created successful life experiences. My paper received a failing score as it lacked proper studies or scientific evidence. I was quoting my grandmother's front porch wisdom talks along with citing positive results when I activated the attitude of gratitude and the feeling of gratefulness in my heart. The failing score brought me to a deeper appreciation in realizing both my grandmother and I were way beyond the times when it came to gathering evidence in our life laboratory for teaching spirit of heart and the wisdom of soul.

I am forever grateful for the time I spent on my grandmother's front porch swing absorbing her lessons of heart wisdom words, intuitive guidance and uplifting energy; especially during the most uncomfortable phases of adolescence. I've practiced faithfully my grandmother's philosophy of "Gratitude is the foundation law of loving life," and experienced it multiplying much success, happiness and fulfillment throughout my life and career of service.

My hope for humanity is to embrace the feeling of gratitude in their hearts as the "law of loving life" for experiencing their own multiplication of abundance, happiness and joy; and to create their own front porch swing opportunities to share heart wisdom and love with one another.

LISA CLAYTON is the founder and President of Source Potential, a human development company, Lisa offers more than 35 years of experience in professional coaching, consulting and training. Lisa created a unique learning method, "learning from the inside out" for developing individual potential with application practices which was used worldwide in facilitator certification programs by clients such as American Express and HSBC.

Lisa conducts intuitive transmissions and counseling sessions as an ordained Angel minister and specializes in connecting individuals with their spiritual gifts. From her passion for heart-focused living, Lisa became a HeartMath® certified trainer and licensed coach. She focuses upon coaching executive levels, management and staff in organizations plus individual clients in reducing stress and increasing heart coherency.

Lisa has creatively combined her intuitive abilities with heart activation and healing techniques to establish the Inner Leader Movement; an evolutionary process for creating successful life situations and relationships that are meaningful, abundant and fulfilling.

Connect with Lisa
lisaaclayton.com
lisa@sourcepotential.com

I am grateful for ...

Week 38

Thankfulness is the beginning of gratitude.

Gratitude is the completion of thankfulness.

Thankfulness may consist merely of words.

Gratitude is shown in acts.

~ Henri Frederic Amiel

HEALING FROM WITHIN YOUR HEART SPACE

For me, finding true beauty of gratitude is when you work to find your sole purpose. I truly believe that it's where you don't let life happen to you, but let life happen for you. Your journey will have twists and turns, but always follow your heart it will never lead you in the wrong way, appreciate how special you really are.

Three years ago, I found my life crumbling before my eyes. My marriage was in shambles, and felt irreparable, I felt like my friends were pushing me aside, and we were in the process of losing our family home. We constantly lived off credit and continued to amass uncomfortable amounts of debt. Our family business that we worked so hard to build up was no longer profitable, and we had no choice but to close its doors. Life felt like a large black hole that was sucking my energy, our finances, and turning me into someone I didn't recognize. I was wrecked by stress, guilt, and feelings of failure.

Finally, after allowing myself to wallow in self-pity, and crying for what felt like, weeks, I did something I hadn't done in a long time. I sank to my knees in my bedroom and prayed. I spoke from the heart, and asked God to help me. I cried out that we were drowning, and that I was so afraid. I explained that I was afraid of the unknown and the lack of direction I felt in my life. I stressed my desire to fix the situation and begged for a sign. Once I was done, I felt peace and strength. I felt relief at having bared my soul, my fears, and deepest emotions. I finally felt safe.

The following day, I had a lunch date with friends. I was hesitant to go as I did not have the extra money for the outing. I was stressed leading up to it, as the thought of charging more to our credit cards was not an option. I scrounged together as much as I could, and ordered the cheapest salad on the menu, and only drank water. This was out of character for me, as before the hard times fell upon us, I was always offering to cover tabs for those who I knew were going through their own struggles.

During the lunch, I shared intimate details of my life and my family's hardships. I was embarrassed and ashamed, but worked up the courage to be honest, as I was really craving some emotional support. Unfortunately, I was met with feelings of ridicule. My friends all but scoffed at me, and not so kindly, told me to stop feeling sorry for myself. They undermined my emotions and at the end of the lunch, I was feeling rejected, deflated, and worn out. I truly felt like I had hit rock bottom and was at the lowest point of my life. It's during the toughest times of your life that you'll get to see the true colors of the people closest to you. However, despite their inability to connect with me on an emotional level, they did offer a piece of advice – get a job. I knew I needed to start somewhere, so I started focusing on where I wanted to go, and not where I have been.

I prayed again, and every night for the next month. I stopped feeling sorry for the person I became taking one day at a time. One night, shortly after myself revelation, I had a dream that spoke to me on a spiritual level. I heard this little voice say, "You silly woman, you and only you hold the power. It's there, deep inside of you. Just find it. Believe in yourself because you have what it takes to pull yourself and your family out of these troubles". When I woke up, I felt refreshed. To this day, I still don't know where that little voice came from, or why it chose that night of all nights to reach out to me, but I knew I had no choice but to listen to it.

The very next day I sat down and made a resume. It wasn't the most impressive, as for my whole adult life, I stayed at home and raised my family. I felt like the qualities that I possessed and the talents I had weren't going to help me in my quest for employment, but in the end, it was all I had. I reminded myself, that no matter what happened, I had reasons to be proud. I had two kind and beautiful children, was a Grandmother to the sweetest young boy, and had a husband who loved and cherished me. At that moment, I let go of any resentment I had been holding onto and started to see my life through the eyes of an outsider. I felt blessed. Being a mother and a wife has taught me many lessons over the years shaped who I am today. Having the support of my family, and the sense of belonging to a winning team made me feel on top of the world.

Shortly after, I went and sent out my resume to many different places around my town, all but avoiding the biggest retail store. I had trepidation about applying there and was almost embarrassed by the thought of it. I had heard rumors and often heard jokes about the type of people who worked and shopped there and had previously decided that it was not the place for me. I quickly shrugged off my ego, that lay over my shoulders like a well-worn in shawl and handed in my resume. Lo and behold, they were the first to get back to with the offers of an interview.

The interview went better than I could have ever imagined, and I was quickly offered a job on the spot. I was so excited and was full of pride. This felt like a huge accomplishment. I was no longer young with my whole life ahead of me. I was middle aged, with no experience other than that of raising a family. Truthfully, after the initial shock of being hired wore off, the nerves set in. I was terrified. I kept experiencing negative thoughts of self-doubt. I felt like it was only a matter of time before I screwed this up. After a week of training, I was officially a retail store associate.

Life had started to feel different for me, and I called on my gut instincts. My life was going places! My angel guides had been pushing me in this direction for many years, but before this time in my life, I was never at a place of acceptance. I quickly realized that I didn't have anything to lose, I had everything to gain.

I also decided to take another leap of faith, and I bought a ticket to a spiritual event with some friends. I took extra shifts at work and scraped up enough money to buy myself a ticket. I went to this event with an open mind, positive attitude, and feelings of gratitude. I quickly recognized a few familiar faces. Women from my gym, work, my neighborhood, etc. Still, I was hesitant, despite the fact that I knew I needed to change the way I looked at life. So, I sat with my peers and listened to everyone share their struggles, and I knew I wasn't alone. I felt an overwhelming sense of belonging and a wave of peace washed over me. I felt at home.

One of the features the event promoted was to win a scholarship for the Goddess Healing System level one. When I first walked in, I was handed the application, but quickly dismissed it as the familiar feelings of unworthiness set in. I didn't feel deserving. However, I did not let that application go. I held onto it the entire event. Right before they were due to be submitted, I decided that I was not going to allow myself to fall back into my old ways, but embrace the change I was struggling too hard to be apart of, I once again heard the little voice tell me that I was worthy, I was deserving and that I needed to do this.

One of the questions on the application was very typical, and asked why should you be chosen for this course? In all honesty, I was stumped. I couldn't figure out an answer. I sat and thought about it over and over in my head, before deciding to just be honest. I answered it with "I don't know who I am anymore; I need to find myself again". I thought of all the things that would help me change my life, and I felt this course was one of them. I laid out my fears, my goals, my concerns, and my desires in a short essay, all the while thinking there was no chance, I would be selected. Just as the event was coming to an end, the winners were set to be announced.

Much to my surprise my name was announced as one of the winners! At that moment, my life took a turn for the positive, and has been climbing ever since. I will always be forever grateful to that event, the scholarship I won, and the opportunity I was given to begin my healing my process. The connection I managed to make with the Universe that day, opened up so much for me and allowed me the release I needed to let go of all the negativity I had been holding onto. I awoke every day with gratitude in my heart which allowed me to face my fears head on. I began to realize that I was enough, and I was worthy - ultimately, I believed in myself again. I felt an overwhelming sense of belonging and a wave of peace washed over me. I felt at home. I will be forever grateful to this amazing lady who opened her heart and believed in me that I was worthy of this scholarship.

Today I can say that I am still employed at the biggest retail store, loving my job. I run an amazing home-based business which allows me to do the crafts that I love. Despite the opposition I have faced as I struggled to get my business off the ground, I know in my heart that one day creating and expanding my home business will be my full-time job.

I will be always be forever grateful for the struggles I've endured in my life, because it led me to who I am today. I no longer cower in the presence of negativity, and self-doubt. Instead, I walk straight towards it with my warrior face on, knowing that I will come out the other side unscathed. My advice to you is to allow change into your life. The choice is yours. Either you let what happened to you define you, or you rise above it. And trust me, the magic truly happens when you choose to the latter.

DAWN SLAMKO is a proud mother of two awesome children, been married for 27 years and grandmother of a phenomenal special needs grandson. She owns a home-based business making one of a kind personal cards for all occasions.

She has been based in or around Calgary, Alberta for most of her life and now resides in Okotoks Alberta. Dawn left home early age of 14yrs and was the only one out of four kids to Graduate High School.

Dawn has always been intuitive knowing things were going to happen before they happen. The last number of years she has been reacquainted with her spiritual side and has really enjoyed studying what the universe and being grateful can do for you, moving forward with challenging times. This has led her to discover that with being grateful with an open heart there are no boundaries at what you can do.

Connect with Dawn
dmslamko@hotmail.com
Facebook @Dawn's Unique Creations

I am grateful for ...

Week 39

Let us rise up and be thankful for if we didn't learn a lot today, at least we learned a little, and if we didn't learn a little, at least we didn't get sick, and if we got sick, at least we didn't die; so, let us all be thankful.

~ Buddha

GRATEFUL AFTER EIGHT:
FINDING JOY AND PURPOSE THROUGH LIFE'S CHALLENGES

My journey began in 1958, on a ranch in Point Reyes Station, a town bordering Tomales Bay in northern California. The ranch was owned by my paternal grandparents. I was a happy, energetic girl who spent much of my time chasing cottontail bunnies and laying in the grass alongside white-spotted fawns as they tried to hide. I longed to touch them, but my Momma had told me not to because their mother would smell human scent and leave them. When I wasn't visiting with rabbits and deer, I hopped around like a grasshopper and flew like a butterfly. Life was good.

One day, while running in the field, I found myself surrounded by a herd of cattle. They started sniffing me, licking me with their tongues. Their noses were a snorting. I was having a perfectly wonderful time, and then I heard my mother's voice.

"Walk slowly to Momma, Vicki…"

As I walked toward her voice, the herd created a path for me to walk through. I felt like a princess! It never occurred to be afraid, at least not until I got to my mom. She wasn't happy with me because I could have been stampeded if the cows were spooked. From then on, I saw the cows while riding around with my Grandpa aka "Pops."

I loved spending time with Pops, and his love for me…well, it was written all over his face every time he looked at me. We would feed baby calves with a bottle. They would suck on my fingers, tickling me and making me laugh. That's how I got my nickname, Ticki. Then we would slip in the bottle nipple into the calf's mouth and watch it guzzle the milk down. Pops would have me count the bottles before and after each feeding.

I also helped out when my dad and uncle milked the cows. I would take the pail to the parlor and they would get it from the tank, then bring it home to Mom. As I got older, I would drive the tractor while Pops cut the bales of hay and fed the cows. My parents eventually went into the sheep business as well. We would get into the 1965 red Jeep and ride up along the mountains to check on them. The baby lambs were so cute, with their long tails bobbing around as they ran.

We always had a beautiful yard, as my mom loved gardening and decorating in a Western theme. We had saddles on boxes and would practice roping with our lassos. Her favorite flower was hanging begonias; her secret was mixing manure to the dirt. We had a chicken coop that she put between the fence and we made it our playhouse.

Our family continued to grow – with one sister born in 1960 and another in 1962. My dad's brother married my mom's sister and their family grew as well. Country life on a dairy farm is pretty quiet until the kids start arriving and to have someone to play with, but my mom kept me entertained too. She was so funny and full of life; a practical joker. She would race me around the house, build tree forts, and she was always laughing.

When I was eight years old, my world changed. I got off the school bus and ran into my house like usual, but the house was empty. Without a word of explanation, Mom put me and my younger sisters in the car and drove away. I remember her face as we turned to go to Petaluma. It was a look that will be with me forever. We arrived at a new house, with a new school, a new everything. Even the milk was different; I was used to getting it from the cows, and now I got it from a carton. It may sound silly, but it was just one more strange thing in my strange new world. Nothing made sense anymore.

My dad did not come around. He would promise, and we'd be sitting by the window waiting for hours. There was always an excuse. We heard he didn't want girls, didn't want us and never asked us to come back. I learned that I wasn't enough, learned what abandonment was all about. I also learned what lack was all about. There was never enough money, and what little food we had, was not the kind we were used to. But Mom was resourceful. Her dad came over and they put in a huge garden. She started canning all the produce so we would have food year-round; she even had us saving our watermelon rinds so she could make pickles from it. I learned to survive. I observed my mom being treated different than the rest of her family. We were all treated different. We were poor. I learned self-esteem, value and judgment. I remember our old car's E brake popped and down the hill it went, into the school fence; I remember cruel kids making fun of us about it. Every day I watched my mom's face fill with stress, then saw her heartbroken when her beloved dad transitioned. I saw her at just thirty-eight years old become very sick with rheumatoid arthritis. It went throughout her body and dislocated all her toes. Eventually she had the bones removed, except the main toe; those she kept for balance.

"I just want to see my girls graduate from high school," she would say.

We made the best of things. My sisters and I would dip her hands in hot wax and peel it off to make funny projects. It always smelled like Bengay, but she was able to move better once the heat hit her joints. Trips to the doctors for gold shots or to have her knees drained of fluid became part of our routine. Acupuncture treatments were pretty cool because they looked like candles on a cake when they were on her back.

As Momma became more crippled people stared at her. You could feel the judgment as you walked through the door to open it up for her.

And still she would say, "Other people have it a hell of a lot worse than us."

How in the world could she say that?

My dad took us a couple times and parked outside the bar. When Mom found out she was furious. Hell no, she said, that won't happen again! She bought my Grampa's 1962 Baby Blue Dodge pickup for $100.00. As each of us grew, we would lift our left arm around the back seat of the sister we sat next to. The passenger side door wouldn't close, so we held it closed with a rope. My mom kept us safe the best way she knew how.

I had my own issues, but I never shared them. What was the point? I had two younger sisters who needed attention, and Mom had so much to deal with already. I learned to stuff my emotions. They had no importance, no value.

Instead, I threw myself into activities, and my energy was boundless. At age nine, I joined 4-H and volunteered to help people. I played guitar, and Mom learned from me. Even though she was crippled she played "Proud Mary" and Tom Dooley around the campfire. I even enjoyed the electric guitar, and went around to convalescent homes, playing and singing to the folks who truly enjoyed it. Some days I'd sit on the porch and in the dairy barn, listening to the music echo off the cement walls. I played sports and exceled as much in the field as I did on the stage. I did so well that no one judged me by my holey shoes or jeans.

I learned to make do with very little. I needed a mitt to play softball and I knew better than to ask. One day, I was walking by a trashcan and saw an old mitt lying in it. It was in terrible shape, but I took it home anyway. I washed it up, laced it up with boot laces, and then stained it with boot stain and marker.

After seeing what my mom had gone through, I decided to go to college. I didn't tell her, though, because I knew she would feel badly about not being able to pay for it. I applied for business school but couldn't get financial aid because my father made too much money. This made no sense! My mother received so little child support. Refusing to give up, I wrote the college a letter; I told them my whole story, how my dad had left us and how we had struggled to make ends meet. In the end I received a grant to attend college. It was a one-year program and when I graduated, no one attended. I didn't want to bother anyone. The familiar feelings of abandonment arose within me again and I just tucked them away.

Mom got a new lease on life when my sons, Matt and Tommy, were born. How she loved spending time with them and imparting the valuable lessons learned over a lifetime: "Be patient;" "Don't get so damn mad;" and "Talk it out." She also loved the expression "slower than a herd of turtle," and was fond of saying, "We have a happy house"; "I got the floor"; and "You get more with honey than vinegar." She also taught my sons how to be excellent cooks and bakers.

On the Tuesday before she transitioned, she thanked me for being there by her side in the earlier years. Then she said the words I will cherish forever:

"I couldn't have done it without you."

Mom became an angel July 20, 2012, which ironically would have been her fifty-fifth wedding anniversary.

She was a great teacher to me and my sons. She taught us more than what you learn in a textbook. She taught love and compassion from her soul. As the journey for me and my sons continues, we know one thing for sure: "Someone else has it a hell of a lot worse than us." I am extremely grateful for my mom and my sons for being such amazing teachers to me!

Who are your teachers?

VICKI ANN MARTINELLI is an authentic, no-bullshit life coach, a successful insurance broker by day and an authentic Reiki Master, Mind-Body-Spirit Practitioner, Certified Angel Intuitive Card Reader, Spiritual Teacher and Ordained Minister by night.

She brings her boundless energy and infectious motivational style to all her workshops and readings, helping others recognize their blessings in the midst of blame. Email Vicki or learn more about her work.

Connect with Vicki
ladyvicki@hotmail.com

I am grateful for ...

Week 40

Happiness cannot be traveled to, owned, earned, worn, or consumed. Happiness is the spiritual experience of living every minute with love, grace, and gratitude.

~ Denis Waitley

EXPERIENCING THE MYSTICAL IN THE REAL WORLD

Know that you can source everything needed to know about life by connecting deeply with any nature spirit or animal spirit, and embracing its wisdom. Each of these beings have lessons to teach us through their actual lifestyle as well as symbolism and metaphors.

Know when you step outside and breathe the air, you can source strength from the natural world. Take a walk on Mother Earth and breathe in her beauty. Her never ending nurturing and reciprocity are all around and guide us in how to serve and love. You will feel better no matter what the challenges or concerns are of the day.

Know that when you sit against or hug a tree these gorgeous standing ones will guide you. You can receive an answer just by asking. Give deep attention and you may feel the energy of the tree's heart pulse through your body.

Know that when you invite the energy of a mountain into the imagination or psyche, you can feel tall, strong, and empowered.

Know that if you imagine flying with a hawk or eagle, you can see your life from a broader perspective or the Higher Self. Your Soul will soar from this bigger picture space, letting go of the mundane details. Truth will come.

Know you can experience each of the elements – earth, air, fire, and water – to cleanse and purify mind, body and spirit. The different forms each give the body and mind choices, so that you may use what you need in the moment.

Know that every time a season transforms and unfolds, it invites you to allow the flow of life's journey. With flow, you can believe everything happens in Divine timing, inviting us to greater growth. Connecting with the energy of a season keeps us aware of all life's diversity.

Know that all parts of Nature can teach us to let go of the past, embrace our life stories as gifts, accept what is, and restore your worth.

Know that, as Black Elk teaches, the Power of the World works in circles – and so everything tries to be round – the earth, moon, sun, seasons, and even birds' nests. This creates the Web of Life.

Know that you are never alone because you are not a separate being from nature or others, but one exquisite piece of our expansive, universal, divine matrix of energy. Nature has an Intelligence that can help us grow, heal, transform, evolve, and love, and you have the capacity to discover all of its magnificence.

Know that Nature and our vast Universe are filled with miracles of divine love and compassion... and so are you in all your glory.

Know that the power and presence of Spirit is infinite and is everywhere.

Please know these Truths. Feel them in your bones as I felt them as a young girl. Climbing the tree in the park, watching the ducks swimming in the pond below, I sensed I was a part of the tree and one with the ducks. I knew this as a child but did not have the words to describe the emotions of my experience. Now as an adult trained in shamanic work, I have experienced that everything is alive and has a spirit, all interconnected in our vast amazing universe. I still may not have the words, but I have the experience, and I believe that it is the fastest way to transformation.

We need not be shamans to experience this mystical web of connection, we need only to be present. We are given the lessons from each being of nature when we pay attention. The more I practice now, the easier it becomes and the deeper my connections manifest. The deeper my connectivity, the stronger my convictions. As my convictions grow stronger, the deeper human being I become. With this depth, my heart is so open, I weep. I weep for the joy of sensing this connection with all beings around me.

Ah, but we are told, "This is not the Real World!" I believe when we enter the world as infants, we know these Truths. We forget them through the process of our life's experiences, challenges and what others tell us based on their world views and experiences.

To live in a place of spirit and divine energy enables us to experience divine mystical moments. If we practice awareness and make time for stillness and introspection, we will receive them.

This is my deepest Knowing. To experience and focus on these holy moments - this is the real world. It brings me strength, harmony, joy, gratitude and blessings. This is our purpose - we must remember that ALL life holds wisdom and preciousness. It teaches love for the world as well as ourselves.

I wish the same for you.

CHRISTINE MOSES MS, Founder of Featherheart Holistic Paths, provides counseling and guidance for personal and spiritual growth as well as the facilitation of women's groups and retreats for integration of mind, body and spirit. As a long-time student and apprentice of cross-cultural traditions and nature-based spirituality, her offerings include many healing traditions. Bridging traditional psychology and intuitive tools with Native American spirituality and healing practices, she supports clients on their journey through transformational work with sacredness and compassion.

Christine holds a Master of Science in Holistic Ministries, is a certified Shamanic Practitioner, Reiki Master, Ordained Interfaith Minister, Ceremonialist, Certified Retreat Leader and author.

Additionally, she trains other women to lead sacred circles. Her book *The Wisdom of Circles: Gathering Women for Conscious Community* is a combination of her personal journey and healing story, a training guide, and an empowering inspiration.

Connect with Christine
chrisfeatherheart.com
christinemoses11@gmail.com
847-525-2600

I am grateful for ...

_____
_____
_____
_____
_____
_____
_____
_____
_____
_____
_____
_____
_____
_____
_____
_____
_____
_____
_____
_____
_____
_____
_____
_____
_____
_____
_____
_____
_____
_____
_____
_____
_____
_____
_____
_____
_____
_____
_____
_____
_____
_____

Week 41

No person, place, or thing has any power

over me, for I am the only thinker in my mind.

~ Louise Hay

BEAUTY IN THE SMALL THINGS

One busy afternoon early in the school year, I opened an email from my dear friend Kim asking me to be a part of a gratitude project she was launching. Intrigued, I chewed on the idea for a bit, then slowly nudged the idea to the back of my mind as I continued with my busy workday. There are many reasons I love and admire Kim, one of which is her uncanny way of gently steering me to take risks when I most need to take them. This was especially true at the time of the creation of her gratitude project. When I received that email, I was not feeling particularly grateful about anything, which was quite unusual for me. I am usually a person who always looks at the bright side of things and understands the power of my thoughts. But as I grew older and the expectations at work increased, I had begun to find it harder and harder to love teaching and to return to work after my adventurous summer vacations. So, after a few phone calls with Kim (during which she applied a little pressure), I found myself dwelling more and more on the idea of gratitude and its role in my life. What kind of gratitude did I exhibit that led Kim to reach out to me? Did I have a story or message of gratitude that I could share that might be something someone - even one person - might need to read? And, quite amazingly, just thinking about gratitude started to bring about change.

First, I was finally moved to purchase Louise Hay's You Can Heal Your Life. This book had been coming up a lot lately; in fact, it was mentioned in three other books I had read in the past month. As I read this incredible life-changing book, I knew it was exactly what I needed to pull me out of the near helpless despair into which I felt I was heading. Underlying Louise's words was a consistent undercurrent of the power of gratitude. Her message of loving yourself and living a life of gratitude inspired me to get back into saying affirmations and more importantly, to spend more time each day thinking about all the things in this world and my life that bring me joy. The more I practiced this, the more I began to notice just the smallest of things.

Walking down the hallway at work one day (we have VERY long hallways), I was alone except for one little girl up ahead who had finished washing her hands and was headed back to her classroom. As I lagged behind her, she very unexpectedly began to jerk her hips back and forth while walking. Apparently, some beloved song must have been playing in her mind for which she could just not refrain from dancing. I watched her with a smile as she strutted her stuff back to class, with no idea that anyone was watching. Not long after, I had just finished working with one of my second-grade groups and was sending them back to class. I watched the five of them start skipping with all their might (skips that trainers call "power skips" and what we adults do for exercise!). Again, I smiled, and as I watched them skip away, I began thinking about why I got into teaching in the first place. When had I forgotten to live by the belief that there is good in everything if that is what you set out to see, and bad if that is what you set out to see? In encountering so many pressing things every day, I had forgotten to stop and notice the joy present all around us. Over time, I had let the seemingly bigger things get in the way and as a result, slowly felt less and less satisfied with my job.

Then, one day while driving home from work listening to music (something I have done a million times before), I was reminded once again of how easy it is to be grateful for the smallest of things. I was thinking about what a particularly beautiful day it was when one of my favorite Pink Floyd songs came across my playlist. Have you ever noticed how some songs just seem to come at the perfect moment? Stopping at a red light, I suddenly became very aware of just how beautiful of a day it was, as I closely listened to the lyrics of the song. I looked out the car window and really saw the sunlight gleaming on the tall grass, which was softly blowing in the light breeze. Seamlessly, I became acutely aware that the beat to the music seemed to be in perfect sync with the sway of the grass and everything at that moment seemed so alive. I am not exaggerating here when I tell you that the beauty of that moment was in such perfection that it actually brought tears to my eyes. Even as I write this, I am happy thinking about it. I believe that moment was meant to bring me back to the awareness of how much gratitude I have for the beauty in this world. I always find my joy in it! But I would have missed it had I not been looking out my window and noticing. This experience inspired me to set a rather ambitious (considering my busy schedule) goal: at least once a month I would go hiking in places where I could spend time in nature, surrounded by things that bring me joy. So, when my daughter called from California to ask me to hike San Jacinto Peak with her the following month, I pushed all fear aside and said yes. (In this alone, there are so many things for which I am grateful.)

On that awe-inspiring drive home, I also started thinking about how when we are in moments of true happiness, there cannot be space for unhappiness at the same time. When we are in an intentional space of gratitude, there is no space for thoughts of jealousy, anger, fear or any of the other unhealthy emotions that bring unhappiness. Try it! Think of someone or something that you are truly grateful for in your life: a child, animal, spouse, sunsets. Go deeper and try to think about the small daily things too- the sound of rain on your roof, a good meal, how happy your dog is when you come home, or a smile from a stranger. While spending time in gratitude, notice how you feel. I have found that the more time I spend in gratitude, the less time I spend being ungrateful for what I have (like a job I am not always thrilled with).

Since I decided to write this piece about gratitude in my life, it has gotten easier to go to work every day and I am happier! Louise Hay wrote in her book about how she spent every morning, before she even got out of bed, thinking about all the things she was grateful for. It is so true that what you choose to see you will see. What would you rather see? Things that bring you misery and sadness, or the things that bring you joy and peace?

Here I am. An author in Kim's gratitude project with a simple message that I am sure we have all heard but often forget: find your joy and see the good and beauty in the world! There truly are so much of both, again, if that is what you choose to see. It is my sincerest wish that you too experience those perfect moments that bring tears of joy to your eyes, and that you experience them every day.

NIKKI DEL BARTO is a wife; mother of three daughters who all continually inspire her for adventure; an ordained minister; and an elementary ESL teacher who passionately teaches English to children from across the world.

She enjoys spreading her motto, "All you need is love" to all that will listen, while continually practicing living a life of love and gratitude in all that she does.

Her passions include health, the humane treatment of all animals and loving and taking care of mother Earth.

Connect with Nikki
Nidelb6828@gmail.com

I am grateful for ...

Week 42

Be thankful for the challenges in life.

For they opened your eyes to the good things

you were not paying attention to before.

~ Author Unknown

WRONG TURNS

It may sound funny, but my gratitude lies, not in the things that have gone perfectly in my life, but in the wrong turns I've made over the course of my journey. What do I mean by wrong turns? I've always believed there are many paths that lead to the same destination. It's up to us which path we take -- some are easier than others — and we oftentimes don't see the bigger picture until we arrive at our destination and reflect back on the voyage.

Think about all the times you have said, *Things would have been so much easier if only I had done this instead of that, had gone faster instead of slower* ... and so on and so on. It's easy to look back and see our mistakes or notice how things might have turned out if we'd made a different decision. But what about the journey? Isn't that what life is really all about?

My favorite poem has always been *The Road Not Taken* by Robert Frost:

Two roads diverged in a yellow wood,
And sorry I could not travel both
And be one traveler, long I stood
And looked down one as far as I could
To where it bent in the undergrowth;

Then took the other, as just as fair,
And having perhaps the better claim,
Because it was grassy and wanted wear;
Though as for that the passing there
Had worn them really about the same,

And both that morning equally lay
In leaves no step had trodden black.
Oh, I kept the first for another day!
Yet knowing how way leads on to way,
I doubted if I should ever come back.

I shall be telling this with a sigh
Somewhere ages and ages hence:
Two roads diverged in a wood, and I —
I took the one less traveled by,
And that has made all the difference.

One could certainly say I've taken the road less traveled, and even what some might consider to be some very challenging detours. At just eighteen years old I decided to hit the road, leaving the comfort of my small hometown in Michigan to start a new life amidst the hustle and bustle of South Florida. Things definitely would have been easier if I'd stayed put in the Midwest, attended college right out of high school and started my career. I'm not sure what my life would look today, but I do know I would have missed out on many priceless experiences and lifelong friendships. All the fun we had together, and all our bad decisions turned out, in hindsight, to be character-building exercises. Although I struggled to make it on my own, and made my share of mistakes in the process, a more comfortable path wouldn't have led me to the valuable lessons and, more importantly, the independence I enjoy today.

So today, I am thankful for the wrong turn that led me to stand firmly on two feet and taught me how to survive on my own.

Throughout my twenties, I explored a plethora of various vocations, searching for something that fit because I didn't yet know enough to honor the calling within my heart. Instead, I was in survival mode, looking to do whatever would keep me afloat and bring in the most income. Yet all those vocations sure built up character and left me with a wealth of knowledge and experience. Through it all, I always remained the curious student, and collected enough certifications to fill an entire wall at the Taj Mahal! I still sometimes wonder what all those certificates really mean. Are they just pieces of paper in a box somewhere? Or, are they perhaps pieces of the puzzle that made me who I am today? Either way, I am grateful for them.

At thirty, I picked up stakes once again and fled an abusive relationship, ready to make a fresh start. After a decade in South Florida, I now found myself starting over alone in a town where nobody knew me, trying to figure out my life purpose. It was here that I started on my spiritual path and began doing the inner work that ultimately nudged me to follow my heart and go to college to pursue a degree in English and Creative Writing. Many ridiculed me and said I'd never do anything with that degree and I was just wasting my money. Two years into my studies, I started my company, Transcendent Publishing, and today I have the honor of helping make dreams come true for aspiring authors all over the world.

While it's never easy to look back on a bad relationship and see the blessing in it, today I can find the gratitude for it. Without that wrong turn, I wouldn't have found my forever home in the arms of a loving husband, in a town where I have many friends and I live in joy every day. For it is here that I had the courage to follow my passion and start my business doing what truly makes my soul come alive. It is here that I finally found my calling and my tribe.

All this leads me to wonder: if I could do it over again, would I change my path? What if I had gone straight to college out of high school? If so, I could have started my company years earlier. But would I have? What if there aren't many roads that lead to the same destination, after all? What if each decision we make affects everything thereafter? Where would I be today if I had taken the shortcut instead of the scenic route? Would I have ultimately ended up where I am now? Or would I be a completely different person in a completely different place?

I may never know those answers, but merely asking the questions makes me realize that I wouldn't change a single thing. Every "wrong" turn, every lesson, every heartache along the way has made me the strong, independent woman I am today. Yes, I may have struggled more than I needed to at times, and I can see now how things might have been easier had I made different choices, but I took the road less traveled by, and that has made all the difference.

What wrong turns have you made in your life? Can you find the gratitude in them?

SHANDA TROFE is an independent publisher and author coach specializing in book-writing and marketing strategies for authors, coaches, healers and entrepreneurs.

Her passion lies in helping those who are called to share a message with the world to find their voice and connect to their authentic, heartfelt story. She believes that a life rich with experience makes for a great message, and she enjoys working with authors throughout the entire process, from idea to publication.

As the Founder of Spiritual Writers Network and President of Transcendent Publishing, Shanda has been helping authors realize their writing and publishing goals since 2012.

She is the bestselling author of several books, including *Write from the Heart* and *Authorpreneur: How to Build an Empire and Become the AUTHOR-ity in Your Business.* Shanda resides in Saint Petersburg, Florida with her loving husband and their two fur babies. You can learn more about her work by visiting her website.

Connect with Shanda
ShandaTrofe.com
TranscendentPublishing.com

I am grateful for ...

Week 43

Gratitude for the present moment and the

fullness of life now is the true prosperity.

~ Eckhart Tolle

START WHERE YOU ARE

He kissed me on the forehead and left for work. Only this time, he never came back. Blindsided and betrayed, alone with two small children, I was confused and deeply hurt. My world flipped upside down in an instant. I was fearful and worried. I'm the kind of person that needs a plan. I need to know where I am going, how I am going to get there, who's going to be there, and what I am going to do once I am there - and then, I need to have five different options just in case something happens so that I'm prepared and don't get caught off guard. So now what? I didn't plan for any of this. I had no idea what to do.

What I did know was that, I had choices.

My first choice, as I saw it, was that I could be bitter, or I could be better. And whichever one I chose would determine the direction that my children and I took moving forward. I chose to be better. I knew that I had to be my best self and the best Mom I could be because I wasn't going to let this disaster define who I was or how my children grew up. But I still didn't know what to do next.

Slowly, but surely, I started to find myself again. I surrendered everything that I thought I knew and asked for guidance, support, and strength. It was in that surrender that I found the power of gratitude! It was also during that time that I learned that I just needed to start where I was. I didn't need to have the entire route mapped out and five "just in case" contingency plans. I just needed to start.

The most radical shifts I've experienced in my life are rooted in gratitude. When I was able to see the blessings and uncover the goodness that was all around me, I started to feel better and positive things started happening for me. In the beginning, the joy I saw was as simple as the sun shining on my face, or that the baby didn't throw up all over me, and that I had a reliable vehicle to take us to our appointments at the children's hospital. I replaced my tattered and worn journal, full of swear words and negative emotions, with a gratitude journal that I wrote in every night after I crawled into bed. I started with a list of five things I was grateful for that day. I'm not going to lie; there were some days that I had to dig really deep and think about what was good. One night I was just grateful that I had made it through the day.

Within a few weeks of this practice, I had a list of 10, and then 20, and then 30 things that had brought me joy during the day. My sleep improved, I began eating again and my energy started to return. My confidence was coming back, and I found I could make decisions again. I was more optimistic and hopeful in the choices I was making and what the future might look like. My spirituality really kicked in and I was able to see more beauty in every day. Finally, I was able to give more love to others and most importantly, to myself. Looking back, I am amazed by the amount of peace that I felt in spite of my difficult circumstances.

I have learned that gratitude is an awareness of life presenting you exactly what you need - whether it be people, circumstances, challenges or obstacles. I learned to trust my path because I was right where I need to be. I learned that gratitude isn't hard - it's simply noticing the good that is already in your life and being thankful for that. I learned that what I focus on is what I attract - if I concentrate on the good stuff then that is what I will receive. If I focus on the bad stuff, then that is what will be present in my life. I have also learned that I can change my day simply by changing my perspective. Living in a past full of regret or a future full of worry would not be living my best life - living in the present is the only place I feel joy and contentment.

Don't worry if you don't know where you are going, how to get there or even where to start. You don't need to know that. Let go of what happened in the past - you can't change it now. Don't worry about the future, you will make yourself sick with what is yet to come. Know that it's okay to struggle - trust that it is part of your path. Open your heart to the goodness that is around you right now. Feel the warm sunshine on your face and the cold, wet rain on your lips. Be thankful for the dishes piled high in the sink because there was food on them a minute ago, and they represent nourishment and love for your body. Fall in love with the crow's feet and wrinkles etched in your face as they are evidence of the laughter and joy you have shared. Embrace the noise and the toys because they represent the children that love you. Appreciate the simple kindness when someone smiles at you in the grocery store, or when they linger for a few moments and hold the door open for you, or they let you skip ahead of them in the pickup line at school. You are worthy. Allow yourself to feel the gratitude as you return these acts of kindness without expectations or strings attached. Practicing gratitude is one of the most important habits that you can develop. It will shift the way you think and feel and gives you a starting place to change your life. I know this because it changed mine!

Start where you are. You got this.

NIKKI GRIFFIN is a certified Autism Travel Professional who owns and operates Divine Wanderlust Travel agency in Calgary, Alberta, Canada. Since embarking on her gratitude journey, Nikki has found and married the love of her life and finds joy each day with her super witty 13-year-old son, and her hilariously funny 15-year-daughter who is on the autism spectrum.

Nikki's passion is helping everyone experience the magic of travel, particularly families with special needs! She believes that everyone should be able to travel regardless of their ability because travel is the best education you can receive.

Nikki is also a certified Access Bars Facilitator and offers life changing sessions that clear the limiting beliefs that hold you back from living your best life. How can it get any better than this?
Boost your brilliant self, engage your sense of adventure, and enjoy a more fulfilled life!

Connect with Nikki
nikki3griffin@gmail.com
Facebook @nikkigriffin or @divinewanderlusttpi.
1-587-439-2626

I am grateful for ...

Week 44

When you are grateful, fear disappears

and abundance appears.

~ Anthony Robbins

JOURNEY TO GRATITUDE

My life changed forever in late 2015, a few months after we listed our house and just before Christmas. It was the end of a long day, and my family and I were in the living room, looking forward to a quiet evening of watching TV and spending some time together. Suddenly, I stood up and fell over, convulsing and throwing up. Frantic, my family immediately called 911 and performed CPR on me until the ambulance arrived. When it did, I was rushed to the closest hospital, where doctors determined I had a ruptured aneurysm - a potentially fatal condition – and immediately sent me to another facility that had neurologists on staff. They performed a life-saving surgery, then placed me in a medically-induced coma. I woke from that on December 26 – Boxing Day in Canada - not understanding or remembering anything of the events that had landed me in the hospital. This was the beginning of a very long journey for myself and my loved ones.

The aftereffects of the aneurysm were terrifying; I no longer knew how to climb the stairs and was unable to recollect the simplest things. My balance was a mess, though with physical therapy, practice and lots of patience, I eventually grew stronger. The worst part of the whole ordeal was the panic attacks; I had never had them before and could not believe their awful intensity.

Despite the many challenges and extremely difficult days, I found myself overwhelmed with gratitude for the doctors and nurses who had saved my life. I was also incredibly grateful to my family for all the support they provided me, and especially for making Christmas at our house even though they didn't know whether I would ever make it home.

My aneurysm changed me, not only physically but emotionally as well. Counselling helped somewhat, but as I would learn, time and patience would be the real healers. This event of course had long-lasting effects on my family too. We had to learn to love each other for who we were NOW. This was not always easy; the trauma had changed each of us, and oftentimes, in ways the others didn't like. It took some time, a lot of frustration and many difficult conversations, but eventually we began to embrace each other again. We knew that we were blessings to each other and that we were worth fighting for. The key here was to understand that we had to grow together along our healing journey.

Incredibly, this seeming tragedy catapulted me onto a spiritual journey as well. I found myself drawn to courses to become an Angel Empowerment Practitioner and a Higher Priestess Practitioner. These in turn led me to tools such as meditation and journaling, which allowed me to reach greater levels of self-awareness. It took a lot of work involving self-reflection, forgiveness work, and most importantly self-love. These courses were journeys in and of themselves, taking me on an emotional rollercoaster through anger, jealousy and resentment toward others who I believed were not living in the present moment, were taking their own lives for granted, or were not "spiritual enough." It was in doing my own inner work that I realized I needed to let all that stuff go. It is not my right or my business to judge anyone else's journey; the lessons they are to learn, or the timeframe in which they are to learn them.

The realization was this was actually one of my greatest lessons. We all have a path, and we can travel it through gratitude if we so choose. What's more, my story, my truth, has finally set me free to live in gratitude and shine my light as a beacon for others to shine theirs.

Choosing gratitude one day, one moment at a time, has opened so many doors for me, each leading to its own beautiful path. Self-discovery through gratitude fills my cup to overflowing, so that I may serve as a way-shower, helping others know they are worthy of so much more. These days, I even embrace the inevitable ups and downs in my life, because I understand how I can use gratitude to navigate my emotions.

We are all figuring life out as we go, and the road is often difficult to travel. Knowing we are not alone helps us in times of struggle, and that is why I share with you my journey, so that you may take comfort in it. Before the aneurysm, I had manifested the life I thought I wanted. It turned out, though that the Universe had other plans; that's why it stopped me in my tracks and sent me in a different, challenging, and ultimately beautiful direction. Whatever your circumstances, I hope you will find the same beauty along your path.

Many blessings to you!

SELENA URBANOVITCH is an Angel Empowerment Practitioner and a Higher Priestess Practitioner. She has also been a hairstylist stylist for over twenty-eight years, eleven of them as the owner of her own business. In her spiritual practice, Selena uses her gifts, not only to heal and empower herself on a deep level, but to assist in creating a world where everyone can realize their interconnectedness with each other, see the value in their dreams, and reach for the stars.

Her goal is for all of us to feel worthy of a beautiful life — both inside and out. Currently, she is developing her own line of products designed to support people along their journey, whether they are connecting with their guides or discovering their inner truth and wisdom.

Selena lives with her husband and two beautiful children in Calgary, Alberta.

Connect with Selena
selena.urbanovitch73@gmail.com
Facebook @ selena.urbanovitch73

I am grateful for ...

Week 45

Gratitude is born in hearts that take

time to count up past mercies.

~ Charles Jefferson

PEARLS OF GRATITUDE

It seems in the past few years, gratitude has become quite the buzzword. It can be found on home décor items, t-shirts and bumper stickers. You can see "thankful, grateful, blessed" blazoned on everything from serving trays and jewelry, to towels and wall-hangings. Despite the message being in front of us almost continually, there seems to be a shortage of people who live as if they truly understand it. What does it really mean to live a life where gratitude is the hallmark of someone's daily attitude? Is it even possible to be such a person? When you stop and think about what gratitude means beyond a catchy phrase, it opens into a pretty deep pool of thought. As I considered this, I came up with a few 'levels' of gratitude I have observed over the years.

Level One Gratitude: Being thankful for family, friends and stuff. This is where gratitude and cultivating a lifestyle of gratitude can begin. Most people have at least some of this quality - there are people in our lives who we love and appreciate, for what they mean to us relationally, for the care and support they give us, and for the basic needs that are met; such as food, housing, or clothing. We can be grateful for our job, even if we don't love it. We can feel grateful for a coworker's help on a tough project, or a stranger who lets you go first in line at the store. When we take time to appreciate the things which are easy to assume and take for granted, to realize the many ways someone's day can be changed by those 'little' things, it can make us want to repeat the experience more often.

Level Two Gratitude: Being grateful for escaping or evading some peril or adverse circumstance. Many of us have felt the intense relief in the near miss of an auto collision, the happy tears of a medical test resulting in a healthy diagnosis, or the recovery from a serious circumstance or life event. To me, this is something felt at a deeper level, because you know what the opposite result could have meant - something life-altering or ending, a no-going-back kind of result. Dodging the proverbial bullet. Your get-out-of-jail-free card getting punched. The angel of death passing you or a loved one by. These events and circumstances are remembered vividly for years and spoken of as often as someone will listen, perhaps with tears of joy and remembrance.

Level Three Gratitude: Knowing in your deepest heart, even in the midst of hard times and terrible circumstances, there is something to be grateful for, and there is still joy to be found, even when you are unable to see it at that time. For this one I will share my personal story with you.

Back in 1984, I was 8 years old, growing up in a happy family with my mom, dad, younger brother and sister. My dad was a speech pathologist for five small school districts in eastern Colorado, and as such, traveled weekly between the various towns and schools. One snowy January night, he was late getting home from work, which was unusual for him. We finally ate dinner, and my mom kept getting quieter and quieter, trying to keep us from noticing her growing fear. About 8 PM, there was a knock on the front door, and a State Trooper told my mom there had been an accident involving a jack-knifing semi-truck, and my dad had not survived. In just a few minutes, everything I had known as a secure, happy child changed. I know, this doesn't really sound like a gratitude story yet, but hang in there.

We missed our dad terribly, but all of us tried so hard to help make things easier for my mom. My mom is my hero, and I could write a whole chapter just on her and how she has done more in her life than some people I know who haven't even had those type of challenges. She deals with an incredible amount of pain every day but hasn't let it keep her down. She had polio when she was 2 years old, lost the use of her legs, and since then, has walked using braces and crutches. My mom had been an elementary teacher before she had us. Amidst all the other chaos of wondering what was going to happen to us and why did this happen to us, was the even scarier thought that we weren't going to have her with us anymore either if she had to work. Six months later, my mom made the decision to move us back to Ohio where her family lived. She devoted her time and energy to caring for us, being both mother and father to the three of us children.

Moving on to my early twenties. My mom, who was always interested in new things and loved helping others, organized a mission trip to the garbage dumps of Mexico City. I reluctantly decided to go with her, my siblings and a group from our church attended as well. At the time, I would have preferred staying home and hanging out with my friends at the pool!

We were joined by another team from California. Imagine my surprise when one of those California guys ends up being the love of my life. One year and two months later, we were married, and I moved out to Northern California. Five years later, we decided to move back to Ohio to start a family. This was an area where we ran into some roadblocks, eventually we began exploring the idea of adoption. One day, as I was ringing up a customer in the book store, I noticed a pin on this lady's jacket that said 'Mary Kay'. I asked if she were a consultant because I didn't know anyone in this area, she said yes, and we became good friends. She and her husband were also in the process of adopting, we decided to work with the same adoption agency. Many hours of classes later, we got the call - there was a nine-year old little boy who needed an emergency placement. We immediately said yes, and today, that broken-hearted, scared, nine-year old little boy is a pretty amazing twenty-two-year-old who we love more than anything. He came to us through his own set of horrible circumstances … which is another chapter yet!

One day we were talking, and he asked how we knew we were supposed to adopt him and not 'some other kid'. This is what I told him: There were too many events and circumstances in all our lives which could have resulted in too many other outcomes for this to be anything other than God ordering our steps all along. And it's even bigger than just this one incident.

Back to 1984. My dad was killed instantly in a car crash. With a semi. Not really a whole lot of mystery as to the cause of death. For some unknown reason, an autopsy was performed. I didn't know this till my late teens, but my dad had an undiagnosed heart condition - the kind of condition you read about when a super in-shape college athlete falls over dead from a heart attack. My dad was not a super athlete, and so never experienced issues with his heart when he was younger. The coroner told my mom he would have suffered a massive heart attack in the next few years and had he somehow survived, would have been left in a vegetative state. In 1984, my dad, despite having a Masters, made about $1000 a month at his job. He hadn't worked long enough to accrue much retirement, and they had only a small life insurance policy. The semi-truck driver who was involved, but not at fault in the accident, was not legally required to do anything for our family. But he and his dad, who owned the company, put together a hugely generous settlement which took care of us and allowed my mom to stay home with us while we were growing up. Had my dad died of a heart attack, we would have had nothing, and my mom would have had to try to work full time while dealing with chronic pain and raising three kids. The alternative of months or even years of seeing him in a coma with no hope of recovery would have been even more awful than him passing.

If we hadn't moved after my dad died to be with my mom's family, I would never have been on a mission trip in Mexico City at the same time as my amazing future husband. I would then never have moved to California and back to Ohio and had a conversation with a make-up lady in a bookstore which led us to adopt a little boy who was from California and was only in Ohio due to some very unique circumstances. He most likely would have ended up in multiple foster care placements or a group home because of his age. When I stop and think of all the other places and people each of our lives could have involved if even one thing had been altered or happened at a different time, it is humbling and fills me with a deep sense of awe and gratitude. Soul deep. So many people who are special to me, beyond even just my family, I would never have known and things I wouldn't have experienced.

Could I have been just as happy somewhere else with different people around me, different extended family members, different friends? Probably, but also not guaranteed. When I think of the hard times we all go through, which seem to have no purpose, no good reason, and we wish we could change or avoid - it brings me up short to realize something; if those hard times go away, so do hundreds and hundreds of good times and precious memories. Growing through pain and adversity is never enjoyable, but by cultivating a spirit of true gratitude and thankfulness for those hard times - not just that we got through them - but for them, creates a mental shift in how we view life. No one wants to be a paraplegic or a widow or lose their parent or struggle with infertility. No one asks to experience loss, illness, or financial struggles. Allowing those times to be seasons of growth and having renewal come from them, makes the struggle not have been in vain. In some cases, the true lesson of a struggle may not be fully understood for years, but even knowing there is a lesson, and that one day we will see it, can be ballast on a stormy sea. Hold tight to that truth and begin to cultivate those small pearls of gratitude in your life - each day - I promise you will begin to see events and happenings in your life in a completely different way. There is most definitely a connection between soul-deep gratitude and true, inner joy that shines through in spite of the darkest times. We just need to hold on to the truth of that until we get there.

HEATHER STRICKLAND is a certified Master Health coach through the Dr Sears program and as of June 2019 will be nationally certified. Her passion is to help people discover ways to improve their health. She is an avid reader and health advocate and loves to dig in and find ways to encourage people in their pursuit of wellness. Her dream is to open a center where all types of alternative medicine, health treatments and pursuits can take place under one roof.

Connect with Heather
stricksolutions.com

I am grateful for ...

Week 46

Be thankful for what you have, you'll end up having more. If you concentrate on what you don't have, you will never, ever have enough.

~ Oprah Winfrey

ATTITUDE OF GRATITUDE
(aka MY SWITCH)

Gratitude for me is what I like to call the flip of my switch. I can go from a pretty self-centered, selfish, and on-the-pity-pot woman to a God-centered woman with a service mind and helping others attitude using a simple process I'd like to share with you. I learned this process a few years ago when my world became very small. You could say I hit an emotional, spiritual and physical bottom. What happened next is life changing. When I reached out for help (extremely hard for this ego-based woman to do), a woman reached back and extended her hand.

This woman asked me to make a gratitude list of at least five things I am grateful for. My response was "What on earth do I have to be grateful for? Are you kidding me?"

To which she gently asked, "Karen, do you have a roof over your head?"

I thought for a minute … really?? "Of course, I do."

Her next question was, "Karen do you have your own bed to sleep in?"

My response again, after thinking a minute on this one, was, "Well, of course I do."

Then she asked, "Do you have your very own toothbrush?" And I started to see where she was going with this. I told her that, yes, I did (understanding that this is truly a luxury for some people).

Her next question was, "And do you have food in your refrigerator?" To which I again replied yes, although this time my throat was tight and my eyes leaking.

I realized that day how truly blessed I am, for by the grace of God, there go I (homeless or helpless or both). I began making daily lists of gratitude.

- ♥ Now when I find myself in a rough spot and need my switch flipped on, I begin something like this:
- ♥ Thank you, God, for the amazing beautiful sunrise I was able to see today from my beautiful back porch.
- ♥ Thank you, God, for the warmth of the sunshine on my face.
- ♥ Thank you, God, for the priceless peace of mind I do have today.
- ♥ Thank you, Thank you, God, for my health and the health of my precious family.
- ♥ May I thank you, God, for the amazing beautiful people that cross my path today that I may help.
- ♥ May I thank you, God, for the amazing beautiful people that cross my path today that may help me.
- ♥ May I thank you, God, for helping me to remain humble and teachable today.

KAREN HETRICK is the creator and owner of Heaven Scent Angel Sprays LLC. Karen is also certified angel card reader and Reiki Master. Her purpose on this earthly plane is helping others to connect with the angels and has created Angel Sprays to assist with their experiences.

She teaches others that angels can; feel, hear, and know us, and that they are always supported by the Heavenly Realms. She will tell you, that it is important to call upon the angels, they are legions just waiting to assist you in all the ways in our daily lives.

Connect with Karen
Heavenscentangelsprays@gmail.com
Facebook @ Heaven Scent Angel Sprays LLC
Phone: 209-404-7960

I am grateful for ...

Week 47

Nothing is more honorable than a grateful heart.

~ Lucius Annaeus Seneca

CELEBRATE THE GIFTS IN LIFE'S SHIFTS

Life is an amazing and wonderful adventure. We all walk through moments of immense joy and experience moments of sheer pain as well. Each moment helps to mold, shift, and transform our lives. One of the biggest gifts or shifts that we experience in this life, comes in the forms of the birth of a new baby, or in passing of a loved one.

Often, we celebrate birth, and mourn death. What if we could begin to shift that experience? For many of us, death is feared. It is a taboo topic no one really wants to speak of. Until it is staring us in the face, leaving us no other choice, but to come to terms with the reality of its presence. For no one leaves this life without dying ... there is no one way pass to becoming a human, we each selected to take the round-trip ticket.

It's never easy to say goodbye to a loved one, sometimes a passing comes sudden without a moment's notice, leaving confusion and shock. And even when we know a time of transition is coming, we can prepare all we want, it doesn't make it any easier. When someone we love passes it often leaves a wound or a hole, a part of us may feel like it's missing or broken, our very foundation may feel shaken.

What if we could see this passing and transition as a celebration of life? Taking time to truly honor our loved ones, their life and accomplishments. Taking time to thank them for a life well lived. Realizing and honoring that life is eternal. The only death is that of the physical body. The soul lives on eternally. I recently read a quote that said, "Death is like removing an extremely tight shoe at the end of a very long day" Unknown, I can so resonate with that!

My Mother passed exactly two weeks ago. And it has led to a whirlwind of emotions. Moments filled with tears in awkward places, wanting and needing so much time alone, to strangers who had no idea of my circumstances coming up to say just the right thing. Emotionally, my Mom's passing lead me to not be able to make a single decision for days on end, unable to eat, and saddened to a level which I have never felt before. My Mom was the one in our family who brought everything together, the one who made Holidays happen, and who gave me life. Our earthly dynamics were not always easy, in fact we were about as opposite of two human beings as we could be. Yet, I loved her immensely. She taught me so very much from how to be, to how not to be. Both equally important and for each lesson I am so grateful! There is a song from the theatrical production Wicked, that sums up this experience quite well, it is called FOR GOOD. In it some of the lyrics are "So much of me is made up of what I learned from you, you will be with me like a handprint on my heart. Because I knew you, I have been changed for good." It's become my daily mantra and have played it over and over each day to heal and get through this time.

In this time of transition, death has an interesting way to bring us to our knees and help to process everything we piled on over the years, whatever we stuffed or suppressed inside finds its way out, seeping through tears. Yet, it's also filled with so many blessings if we can begin to see them. Death can also help us to arise from the ashes and begin anew... it has a way of helping us to appreciate the little moments, to slow down and breathe life in. It can make the first crisp morning after months of 100-degree days in Phoenix, feel like a miracle. After days of not being able to eat and having no appetite, to sipping my first iced eggnog latte tasting like heaven in a cup. Watching my beloved nap on the couch yesterday brought me to tears. The simple joy of watching two little girls play in a park, dance to music, and blow their bubbles becomes a magical and sacred moment I am so grateful to witness. Meaningful conversations with friends and loved ones take on a whole new meaning as we can begin to appreciate their very presence in our lives.

Even my feelings around butterflies are completely transformed. I have always loved butterflies, and now since my Mom's passing butterflies are coming to me daily. I believe as a symbol of transformation. See, my Mom earned her wings as they say, and is now dancing through her next chapter of life healthy, and freely. I have begun to see life a little bit deeper, a little sweeter and a little more sacred in its daily moments and interactions. With each butterfly's visit I have another moment to forgive, to heal, and to think of a good memory with my Mom and am reminded there is only love. Forgiveness has the ability to transform the pain, to heal the hurts of the past, and to let go of any underlying wounds. Love truly does have the power to heal and transform all areas of life if we let it.

I am encouraging you to take the time to connect with loved ones both present and even those who may have passed or just moved physically out of our lives. Let them know how much they mean to you, tell them now how they have molded and shaped your life. None of us are guaranteed tomorrow. Please know, if someone has moved on or is no longer physically present in your life, you can do this on a spirit level. Simply bring this person to mind and see an image of them in front of you. Begin to speak anything in your heart being sure to stay centered in love and forgiveness. On a spirit level there is no time or space, they will receive your message.

Inviting you to join me to experience the gift's in life's shifts ... let's love fully, completely and without limits. For love, gratitude and forgiveness lead us to our next chapter and new beginnings in life, for ourselves and for all those around us.

May you always see the gifts in life's shifts as they surround you.

With Love & Gratitude,

Elizabeth

ELIZABETH HARTIGAN is The Gratitude Girl, Founder of Creating a Life in Balance; an author, speaker, and coach.

Helping amazing and beautiful beings get from where they are to where they want to be by offering courses, coaching, and products to bring more balance to life. Elizabeth helps you dream big, dare greatly, and take inspired actions and move through life's transitions! What are you being called to create or step into? Elizabeth can help you put together a plan and inspire you to get there!

The entire book: *Experiencing The Gifts In Life's Shifts* is in the works and coming soon.

Connect with Elizabeth
TheGratitudeGirl.com
928-963-1057

I am grateful for ...

Week 48

Gratitude is when memory is stored in

the heart and not in the mind.

~ Lionel Hampton

THE CHRISTMAS APPLES

I now know why my grandparents were farmers and why they say God is close to the land. One simple apple tree and my first experience of its harvest forever changed me.

The summer was cool. The tree was pruned well but not sprayed. By Labor Day, it was heavily laden with green and slightly red apples. I anxiously picked some for cooking applesauce, never realizing what prizes awaited. By mid-October the abundance began. My husband and our children and their friends picked them. Our 8-year-old Claire and her friend Erin individually wrapped them in colorful magazine paper for safe storage.

We peeled them, chopped them and processed them. We mixed them into muffins, breads, cakes, cookies, sauces, jams and even apple soup! It was wonderful and tiring to handle them all — but we were a bit obsessed.

We sorted them into bushel baskets "for eating" and "for cooking." Most of them were perfectly shaped and their scent was so fresh! They were crisp, red, sweet and yummy!

Our four-and-a-half-year-old son Christopher, along with his two little buddies, loved picking and eating them. The apple picker was three times their size but together they balanced it.

After fishing the tree with wide eyes and a strong tug, the three little boys would catch their prizes that fell to the grass floor and squeal with joy.

I watched them through the window with delight while I rocked Carly for her nap. Her head alternately rested on my chest and bounced up. She would point to the window and excitedly call out "appas" as I settled her into sleep.

Back in my kitchen, I was inspired by my Aunt Vi, whom I never knew, and her culinary contribution of apple-peach-orange jam. I experimented with recipes too. In our muffins and sauces complimentary flavors included, apple-lemon, apple-grape, apple-raspberry, apple-strawberry and of course we made Aunt Vi's recipe of apple-peach-orange jam. Her recipe was perhaps the most delicious of them all. The peach serves as a bridge between the apple and the orange.

Our children got creative too, when they decorated the jars of preserves for gift giving at our church's Christmas craft fair. We were apple crazy, and I even found a scrumptious border for the kitchen in my new home. The simple border of lattice design with apples and grapes was perfect for my kitchen that I patiently waited to decorate.

My choice for the kitchen decor was influenced by my sister Jane, an Interior Designer, who told me it would be gratifying to decorate my home after living there for a year. Once a year has passed, she advised, the decorating evolves organically from the experiences and personality in the home. This was such good advice because I would always love the apples on that luscious wallpaper border in our kitchen. Even when the Apple tree was bare, the kitchen wallpaper was a symbol for this great experience of our first apple tree. I was so grateful to my sister for her advice and was glad that I waited to decorate the kitchen. I even loved the wallpaper and apple border when they weren't so "in" anymore.

This apple experience continued in our holiday decorations. Along with varied berries, assorted apples adorned our garlands and tree, wreaths and boughs. I wanted to abandon myself to our apple tree, this symbol of God's abundance. I wanted to be wrapped up in apples, to continue to feel their protection.

We felt even more gratitude for our good health! No one was sick in our family that entire winter or spring — not so much as a cold for anyone. With little ones, sniffles and winter seem to go together. I think the "apple a day" adage is too simple an explanation for this good luck. I believe our sheer gratitude for the bountiful harvest from one little apple tree to one family produced enough energy to resist many a "bug" for a long time.

Thank you, God, for your unending blessings in our lives. In this simple experience of enjoying nature's abundance our experience of You was illuminated. You were — and are always — more than enough.

ROSEMARY HURWITZ, a married mom of four young adults, is passionate about an inner-directed life and she found the focus for it in the Enneagram. The Enneagram is a time-honored personality to higher consciousness paradigm used worldwide. She received her Enneagram Certification in an MA. Pastoral Studies program at Loyola University, Chicago, in 2001. Rosemary has studied and taught the Enneagram ever since. She also gives Enneagram-based individual coaching for self-awareness and emotional wellness.

Rosemary has a BA in Broadcast Communication, and Certifications in Intuitive Counseling and Angel Card Reading and uses these wisdom traditions in her spiritual teaching and coaching. For over twenty years, along with her husband, she gave Discovery Weekend retreats, patterned after Marriage Encounter, for engaged couples. She is a Professional member of the International Enneagram Association. Reviews at spiritdrivenliving.com.

This is Rosemary's fifth co-authored inspirational book, and *Who You Are Meant to Be: The Enneagram Effect,* her first single-authored book is coming soon!

Connect with Rosemary
rosepetalmusic@gmail.com
spiritdrivenliving.com

I am grateful for ...

Week 49

I looked around and thought about my life. I felt grateful. I noticed every detail. That is the key to time travel. You can only move if you are actually in the moment. You have to be where you are to get where you need to go.

~ Amy Poehler

TEACHERS

Gratitude comes to us in many different ways; in my own journey I have much to be grateful for, especially as I look back and reflect upon my experiences. What I have observed during the different phases of my life, are the various teachers that have shown up when I felt ready to expand and move forward.

If you look back in your life and remember your school teachers, there are ones that made a difference in your life. For me, it was an English teacher. She accepted me for who I was, the shy, quiet girl. By her accepting me, it led me to enjoy the class itself more, this was a gift because it made the subject come alive for me. I was so thankful for her kindness because in the beginning I was scared and searching for acceptance.

As I have grown older, I've come to have more gratitude for the many teachers that arrived on my path as I became open to learn. When my life was ready for a change it always showed up. I remember the day I received the news, that a neighbor was struggling with her health and it was serious, in fact it was highly possible she was not going to live. I had a disturbing feeling, it caused me to reach out and see what I could do to help. At first, she was only an acquaintance but for some reason I knew I needed to reach out to her. This small intuitive nudge to connect with her, changed my life forever. In the few years that I helped take care of her, I received so much and have tremendous gratitude for the lessons I learned in this experience. The big message was, don't take your health for granted. I also learned so much about the human body, this helped ignite a desire for me to help others. She showed me what keeping the faith really meant. She is still living, and I am so blessed to have her in my life.

When I was ready for a new change, I was introduced to someone who did something called Reiki. It was a life changing moment; I had a couple of treatments and knew then I needed to learn this modality for myself. Eventually that led me to wanting to help others with the gift of Reiki and teaching them how to help themselves as well as working with clients with this beautiful gift. I will be forever indebted to her for teaching me so much about life and such an amazing healing modality.

Right when I thought I had it all figured out, the next teacher came around. She started to encourage me to go deeper within myself for inner healing. I didn't know a whole lot at the time about the mind-body connection, and how emotions affect us, and it was an eye opener for me. That was the beginning of me discovering my truth and finding out who I really was. I always thought I just existed, and that led me to just do what I was told to. It was not easy opening up and showing others my emotions, especially as I was also discovering them. She helped open doors for me to find even more opportunities and experiences to learn more about myself and the spiritual world. I also was introduced to so many amazing people who were like me and accepted me for who I was; this created connections that I know in my heart will last for a lifetime. That is such an amazing gift; I'm so grateful for her showing me love and that I was stronger than I ever imagine.

When it was time for me to reach a new layer of inner healing the next teacher showed up. I noticed this theme emerging of being ready to go forward and a new teacher appearing. I thought I was done with all the inner healing, I was wrong. There are so many layers to our healing processes. She taught me many ways to continue releasing those layers. I will forever be grateful for the caring and listening this teacher has given me. She has taught me I am enough! I can accomplish any dream if I only believe.

There have been many important teachers in my life; as I allowed myself to open, they came in to teach me what I needed at that time. I am beyond grateful for each person and every situation in my life, the good and not so good. I believe this because I know they have all been teachers in one way or another. Be open to be taught and you will be forever grateful for the miracles that show up.

DENA HANSON is a Reiki Master, Access Bars Practitioner and Ordained Minister. She has a passion for helping people and animals heal, especially in nature. Dena loves helping those who are ready to access the light within. She built a labyrinth after experiencing the healing and peace they can hold. Her labyrinth became a personal tool to help herself and others through inner turmoil and struggle.

Dena feels blessed to offer her labyrinth to others. Nature is healing and including the labyrinth into her personal and professional work has transformed her life. It quiets the mind, body, spirit, and allows a person to release, receive and return.

Dena creates a safe place and freedom for people to release physical pain, mental pain and all layers of their journey without judgment. To learn more about Dena's services or to visit her labyrinth be sure to connect with her.

Connect with Dena
Facebook @ Access Your Light
accessbars123@gmail.com

Artwork by Christina Hladnik

I am grateful for ...

Week 50

Gratitude is an antidote to negative emotions,

a neutralizer of envy, hostility, worry, and

irritation. It is savoring; it is not taking

things for granted it is present oriented.

~ Sonjya Lyubomirsky

WHERE WOULD I BE?

In the bleak first days and weeks, it was impossible to imagine anything outside of my grief, shock and sadness. I was merely surviving. I slept with every light on, wading through each day dazed and unfocused, taking hours to complete simple tasks.

Surprisingly, a sliver of gratitude appeared not long after Dad's suicide. I sat down in a café one day to write my dad a letter. In it, I shared my sadness, regret and disappointment about my life with him, but then I thanked him. I wrote about the traits that I'd learned from him, like his desire to put a smile on people's faces – even strangers; he always had a joke to share (typically off-color). And more importantly, his deep compassion for others - like the way he'd take the long way home from work just so he could take sandwiches or snacks to the homeless regulars along the way. I'd spent so long trying not to replicate the chaos of his mental illness that I'd overlooked the most beautiful parts of who he was. In that moment, as my tears poured down and blurred the words on the page, I felt deeply grateful and proud to be his daughter. And there was much more to follow. I had no idea how his life, and death, would alter the course of my own life.

I clearly recall the first anniversary of his passing. I walked to work that cool, gray morning, peppered by the first drops of a storm. I dialed mom's number and was relieved when I heard her familiar voice. You see, I'd laid awake the night before, asking myself if Dad had lived his bravest, boldest, most joyful life - and of course I already knew the answer to that. I'd watched Dad struggle with mental illness my entire life. And that begged the question, "Was I creating my dreams, was I truly living, or merely existing?" And the answer was clear. I wanted marriage, children and adventure – I wanted joy. Instead, I was a single, childless 33-year-old woman, married to the security of a regular paycheck and living an unexceptional life. When mom answered the phone, I told her that I wanted to resign from my career and travel the world. She told me I should do it. There began a year of planning and countless vaccinations, of books about all the dangers lurking in my travel destinations. There were countless mornings that I'd wake cozy under my down duvet, sun streaming in and my sweet cat purring at my feet, where I'd bolt upright, panicked and wonder what the hell I was doing. But a little voice whispered, "You can do it." And my fear of regret was greater than my fear of the journey. So, I did it!

For the first leg of my trip I'd somehow convinced my mom and sister to backpack with me. We visited Southern Ireland and stood under tapestries of our dastardly ancestor, traversed colorful towns and gobbled down hearty Irish breakfasts. In Greece we climbed every crumbling site of interest, travelled to the unfathomably high monasteries of the Meteora Mountains, and watched the sunset in Santorini. In Italy we hiked the trails of the Cinque Terre, admired the ancient art, churches and history, and took afternoon naps to escape the scorching heat. We laughed, we sweat (a lot), and occasionally we bickered, but we sealed a memory that can never be undone. For that I am grateful.

Back in London we shared teary goodbyes and I set off on a three-month camping trip through Eastern and

Southern Africa. It was an eye-opener – the sights, smells, challenges, children and beauty of Africa were forever etched into my heart. I gorilla-trekked in Rwanda; bartered for food in shanty markets; cooked meals over a fire; jumped from a plane over the Namib desert; and walked alongside lions in Zambia, but it was the people and the way they live that created a gratitude for the ease of my life at home.

In the Middle East, specifically Egypt and Jordan, I found myself dangling sideways from a donkey as it raced through the streets of Luxor, while old men smoking hookahs pointed and laughed. I saw pyramids and tombs, slept under the stars on the deck of a Felucca boat while sailing down the Nile. Once, I hiked upward through the dark night, bumping against donkeys and camels, to watch the sunrise atop Mount Sinai. In Jordan I enjoyed the syrupy sweet cinnamon Bedouin tea prepared over a small fire in the beautiful red desert of Wadi Musa. I witnessed the historic Rose City of Petra, but most importantly, I developed a gratitude for my place and rights as a woman in the Western world.

And finally, I headed to SE Asia. In Borneo, I experienced the peace and beauty of the rainforest and took a boat to see the cartoonish proboscis monkeys. In Cambodia, I took in the serene orange-robed monks at ancient Angkor Wat and watched the banana trucks in awe, wheels bulging under their story-high loads. But it was Thailand that calmed me. Though I took in the islands, slurped curry and learned Thai cooking, it was my time alone in a hut on an eco-farm where I was finally still. There was a day that I call my dragonfly day – my greatest stressor was getting the perfect photo of a giant dragonfly. It reminded me to slow down and experience all the magic around me. It was there that I learned gratitude for solitude and calm.

My travelling experience was irreplaceable, but it was about so much more than the sights, animals, cultures, food and adventures … it was the journey I took on the inside, noticing traits and abilities I didn't know I possessed.

When we go where no one knows us we become most ourselves.
~ Author Unknown

Dad's passing created a tremendous ripple in my life. And though I've so often thought about missing out on time with him, and having my children know him, I clearly see him in my youngest son's comedic antics and I get chills looking into my eldest son's eyes – so like his grandpa's. I know that he is here with us.

It seems that gratitude often finds me in the crevices of discomfort, and I guess my lesson has been that we don't know; in the anguish of challenges that we face, we never know what will come of it. We never know if there's an opportunity for growth, or self-love or connection with others.

Where would I be were it not for Dad's passing?

Would I have recognized the beauty in him?

Would I have had the audacity to leave a career I loved to fulfill a dream of travelling the world?

Would I have had the courage to meet my husband and build a family with him?

Would I have created greater connections with my loved ones?

Would I have become outspoken about mental health and suicide prevention?

Would I have recognized how courageous, resourceful and resilient I can be?

Where would I be?

Although I'm not grateful for the actual loss of my dad, I am forever grateful for the incredible ripples it's created in my life.

SHANNON DEANNE, a graduate of Business Management at SAIT and Technical Writing at Mount Royal University, spent ten years as a successful business analyst and technical writer. She took off her corporate hat and donned a backpack to travel the world and has since traversed 27 countries, soaking up cultures and delicious foods.

A passion for writing has led to taking countless creative writing courses and workshops, primarily through Alexandra Writer's Centre Society. Shannon enjoys working with small businesses and individuals on everything from web copy to resume writing.

When she's not perched in front of the keyboard, you'll find her cooking up a feast, on an adventure with her husband and zoo of two boys or sharing messages as a spiritual medium. Be sure to check out her new blog at shannondeanne.com.

Connect with Shannon
shannondeanne.com
shannondeanne.writer@gmail.com

I am grateful for ...

Week 51

Two kinds of gratitude: The sudden kind we feel for what we take; the larger kind we feel for what we give.

~ Edwin Arlington Robinson

FAMILY, FRIENDS AND PRAYER

I have a small notebook beside my bed to remind me each night to write down what I am grateful for. It doesn't matter if I have had a good day or a bad day. I see the notebook and my day starts to flourish through my mind. I begin to think of the blessings that I have had and what I am thankful for. Some days are not the best days, but when you start looking for the blessings, it does get easier. I have done it for so, long, that I am not sure I can fall asleep without writing my gratefulness for the day. I think the whole process is just to start thinking about gratefulness and to write down what you're grateful for, then my mind settles, and I'm full of gratitude. This has not always been a natural habit, but I feel better when I do it.

I live on a small hobby farm by myself and have many animals. I have dogs, cats, ducks, geese, chickens, roosters, horses, miniature horses, miniature donkeys, and miniature mules. One September day I was out on my four-wheeler fixing fence in the pasture, then decided to ride over to the local bar. I had pizza and drinks while visiting with friends. Someone secretly added a drug to my drink. I left and was on a gravel road not even a mile from town when I rolled my four-wheeler. I laid there in the ditch until morning when a nice man that lives along that road saw me and called for help. I was taken by ambulance to the hospital where they discovered I had a traumatic brain injury, along with an injury to my right arm, my left leg was partially numb, and facial palsy. At the hospital, they tested me for alcohol, and it was no surprise that it came up positive. What astounded me was when my test came back positive for drugs. The police decided that somebody at the local bar had slipped something in my drink. I was in ICU with high blood pressure issues and was put on seizure medications. Family members stayed with me for quite a bit of the time. After about four weeks in the hospital, it was decided that I was moving to a nursing home to continue therapy and heal. They told my family that I would probably be in the nursing home for the next five years.

I am very blessed that I had my family and friends praying for me! I am grateful because my family and friends took care of my hobby farm and animals. I don't remember much of the hospital stay, but I do remember the nursing home. At age forty-four, it wasn't a place I really wanted to be, but I needed therapy, and I wasn't well enough to live on my own. The staff was pleasant, and the residents were friendly. I would visit when it was time to eat but then would go back to my room. I had a single room and slept much of the time. I knew I needed to get better and sleeping all day in a nursing home wasn't going to help much. Yes, I needed rest, but I also needed help in the healing process. I was doing therapy at the nursing home and had started practicing Reiki, but I needed to do more. Reiki is a class I took a few years prior to encourage emotional and physical healing. I needed both.

My sister and brother-in-law decided that I could come live with them the end of October, so I was only in the nursing home for about two weeks. Now that's something to be grateful for! They brought my dogs out to their farm, and my sister works from home. The speech therapy really helped the paralysis of my face, and the side of my mouth didn't hang so low. People occasionally asked if I had a stroke or Bell's palsy. My leg still remained numb, but I could walk reasonably well. The arm was getting stronger, but my elbow wasn't quite right. I couldn't straighten my arm out all the way or bend it entirely, and I had lost a lot of strength in my whole body. However, things were improving, and the physical therapy was helping.

My brother-in-law asked if I wanted to help tend the cows. We moved cattle out of the pasture, and it was that time of year to start feeding the cows, so I would open up the gates to the different pens. He had about four hundred head of cattle to feed and the bulls as well. I would also feed my dogs and take them for a walk. I started doing regular chores but was still napping daily. I sure appreciated them letting me live with them. They or my parents took me to my appointments. I wasn't supposed to drive due to the head injury and the seizure medication. I am thankful I never had a seizure, and I was on the medication to prevent one from happening.

I don't remember all that happened, but my family sure has stories to tell me. I was irritable at times, and it seemed like I slept a lot. I missed my home, my animals and my job. My parents had gotten all the horses and miniatures moved to their farm and for that I was grateful. I was thankful my friends took care of them and grateful to my brother-in-law for transporting them. My sister set up an appointment out of state to see a specialist to make sure all the basics were covered, and we were not missing anything. He was an excellent doctor, but that was quite a drive. The specialist agreed with pretty much everything the doctors had been telling me. Although he added no riding four-wheelers, or horses, no alcohol, no caffeine, and no more head injuries, especially in the next two years.

I was doing pretty well and had shown good signs of improvement. The doctor took me off the seizure medication and said I could return to work. He also said I could move home in the middle of December. They were surprised at how far I had come. I had lots to be grateful for! I was excited to go back to work and really excited to move home! The only animals I took back home with me were my dogs and the barn cats that my friends had kept. The doctors didn't want me overwhelmed, so my parents were happy to keep the horses and the miniatures during the winter months.

I applied for unemployment and proceeded to look online for a new job. My health benefits would last to the end of January. I had plenty to do at the farm since I had been gone for about three months. I changed the oil in my International tractor and hooked up the snow blower to it. I went and bought some chickens and a few roosters, so I got my coop all ready. In the spring my horses and miniatures would be coming back home.

I had a couple of job interviews, which didn't work out. I was getting a little disgusted. I was still writing in my gratitude notebook each night and writing objects of thankfulness on my erasable board. I was without health insurance now, so I stopped my therapy for the time being. I had another interview and decided I would apply at a temp agency. On my way to the temp-agency appointment, I was called and was offered the job that I previously interviewed. I accepted the position and now have health benefits.

My family was a big help and for that, I will always be grateful. My friends were right there to help as well. I have said lots of prayers and received many prayers from others. Reiki has helped me heal emotionally and physically. I am grateful for all the help from the doctors and therapists. I am working full-time and doing my home business part-time. I am still healing and will continue to improve. I keep in contact with my doctor. I see a massage therapist and a chiropractor regularly. I am healthier and eat more nutritionally than I have in years. I don't drink alcohol or caffeine. I have forgiven the person that drugged me that night in the bar. I am grateful for the blessings to forgive and accept the healing process. I live on my hobby farm and have all my animals home. I just love it and will continue to be thankful every day!! I will always be grateful for my family, friends, and prayer!

DANA SCHRADER is a positive person and is always recognizing objects of gratitude. Her family is a significant part of her life. She feels guided by her angels and sees the true beauty in her grandchildren. Her friends have always been a gift to her and she loves to visit with them.

She has healed so much since her accident and sees things in an even brighter picture. She is willing to help people and learn from them as well. She believes that the process of journal and burn is a great release that can benefit anyone. Dana believes that honest communication is key to having a blessed life.

Connect with Dana
sign3@rrt.net

I am grateful for ...

Week 52

Gratitude is the sign of noble souls.

~ Aesop

TRANSFORMATION OF THE CATAPITTY
I AM LOVE

On a beautiful spring day many years ago, my daughter came running into the house, excitedly yelling, "I found a CATAPITTY!"

Nina beamed as she pointed to the brown and yellow fuzzy caterpillar crawling up her arm. We put Ms. Catapitty in a mason jar and poked holes in the top for air. At seven years old, my daughter knew that caterpillars transformed into butterflies. She was convinced that she was going to witness a miracle.

My transformation from a fear-based being to one grounded in love is like a caterpillar's story. As a child, I was cute and fuzzy, but kept in a jar. I was the youngest of five in a classic dysfunctional Catholic family in Salt Lake City, Utah. My oldest sibling, thirteen years my senior, went to Vietnam when I was just five. Critically wounded two years later, I went with my family to San Francisco to retrieve him from the VA hospital. At seven years old, I walked the halls of those wards. Gruesome to say the least. Those images were seared into my young brain.

Things did not get better. My oldest sister got pregnant at sixteen. Another sister started down a path of drugs and alcohol. I was only nine, but when Ana came to the dinner table tripping on acid, I instinctively covered for her. I was the protector. Our home fell apart literally and figuratively as we moved from my parents' "dream home" to an apartment. Ana ran away. Mom had a mild nervous breakdown and Dad became consumed with finding Ana.

At twelve, I started to look for a way out of that jar. I picked fights at school, just to see what it physically felt like. I got drunk to the point of passing out, even under my parents' noses. Mom was overwhelmed with depression and grief. My father found my sister and brought her home, sick with addiction and physical ailments. She was sent to the State Mental Institute for rehabilitation. I still instinctively tried to protect her, visiting her every weekend and going on group outings with her fellow "rehabbers."

This extreme need to protect her went on for years. I wanted to make her better, to make my parents see her as the wonderfully funny person that she is. No matter what she was doing, how she was acting, who she was hurting, I defended her because I saw something different than the others did. This was the beginning of what I now know as enabling. And I got good at it.

In our family, Dad went to Sunday mass at the crack of dawn, so he could then go golfing. Mom took us, to a later mass but that stopped by the time we were in the apartment. When I was thirteen, I went to "Jesus Freak" bible studies with a bunch of girls from school. Like all good lil' Jesus' Freaks, I was led to the altar to accept Jesus Christ as my lord and savior. It was the first time in my life that someone told me that "I am love" and that "love" resides in me.

I kept rocking the jar, trying to tip it over so as to execute an escape. I got pretty banged up in that jar; I experimented with drugs, experienced deep depressions, and found boyfriends that liked the fact that I was in the jar and easily controlled. I was the epitome of a co-dependent enabler. I found my purpose in others; I was a warrior for others. I defended, protected and furiously fought for the very people who I allowed to hurt me.

Ten days after high school graduation, I moved to California to be with my boyfriend and Susie, my oldest sister. I had now taken on the duty of protector of her. Susie was living in a self-imposed exile from her children and family, and I had become her warrior. I saw the loving kind motherly sister who held me and wiped away my tears when I was young. Just like with my other sister, no matter what Susie was doing, how she was acting, who she was hurting, I defended her because I saw something different than the others did.

I married at age twenty and immediately prepared to move to Venezuela. I was looking for my way out of the jar and had chosen to go away, far away. One month after my wedding day, I stood on the tarmac at Los Angeles International airport. The crew had let us out there to empty and repack our moving container to see if we could fit our table and chairs. A horse shoe, given to me by my mother for good luck, fell out of nowhere and hit me on the head. Time stopped for a moment. I KNEW that something horrific had just transpired. It had. Susie had been in an accident resulting in severe brain damage.

My jar had smashed, and I was gasping for air. In the ICU standing before a distorted version of Susie, asking for a priest to administer her last rights, I was being asked to make decisions about her imminent death. My parents were in Salt Lake scrambling to find flights to California. My sister's body did not die that day, but the sister I knew and loved did.

I moved to Venezuela to begin to experience life out of the jar. We lived there for five years and I began to play the part that I would play for the next twenty years of my life, with bouts of depression and self-loathing. I had slithered away from the shards of broken glass of my jar to climb a branch and begin to build a wall around myself. I went into the cocoon.

I would have remained in that protective cover, not knowing my potential, not experiencing my perfection and magnificence, if it wasn't for my earthly angels, my teachers, who happen to be my children. I didn't realize it then, but I had created my own dysfunctional family. I had now taken on the duty of protector of my husband. No matter what he was doing, how he was acting, who he was hurting, I defended him because I saw something different than the others did. He too became progressively sicker with his abusive behaviors.

The story started to repeat itself, my son got involved in drugs and alcohol, my daughter suffered from depression, and my youngest, the innocent fuzzy catapitty, watched the whole thing. Me, the warrior run amuck, ran around protecting and trying to fix everything and everybody. I needed to get out of my cocoon. I needed to unravel the threads. I could feel within me it was time to break out and be the butterfly. To be the miracle. The words swelled in me: I NEED TO SEE THE LIGHT! DEAR GOD, PLEASE LET ME SEE THE LIGHT NOW!

On December 27, 2005 my cocoon split open. My husband of twenty-five years physically attacked our daughter who was home from college. It may sound surprising, but that day is now looked upon by my children, their father and me, as a blessed day - a day of awakening. On that day I transitioned, my wings were loosened, and we were all set free.

Within one hour of that incident, I sat calmly in front of my family enveloped with the peace of God, understanding that every moment, every instant in that jar and cocoon was me preparing for this next chapter of my life. I felt deep gratitude. The enabler was now a spiritual warrior.

I realized that I was the only being that needed to say, know, experience, demonstrate that I AM LOVE. Since then I have gone on a wild discovery of self-love. I am on a mission to surround myself with love, to be love, to exhibit love, to be a spiritual warrior for love. My job is now about showing you that you are made of this same light. You too are pure love. We are all catapitties, all in the jar where we can die, or we can create a cocoon to grow strong. Be grateful for the moments that strengthen your wings and allow you to fly free.

We all have our own jar stories. And we all have nothing but LOVE inside us. Right now, take a moment, physically touch your heart, and feel where your true essence resides. Hear your higher self gently whisper in your ear, "I am Love." Know that you are a miracle and know what my daughter knew at seven years old: catapitties turn into butterflies. All is well, it's time to fly. Break free from the jar, break out of the cocoon. Say the words I AM LOVE and soar!

VIRGINIA "GINGER" ADAMS – Master Energy Healer, Intuitive Guide, Author, Artist and Creator of the Universal Gravity Code Program.

Virginia is a well-known motivator and medical practice administrator for over 28 years. Her dedication, integrity, and intuitive nature have positively impacted many healthcare practices and individuals around the world.

Years ago, Virginia received what she feels was a divine mandate to "Heal the Healer". Until that moment, she had described herself as a practical and methodical administrator. The seed planted by that mandate sent her on a path of discovery, ultimately leading to the opening of her Reconnective Healing® healthcare practice.

"Today I stand in immense gratitude for where my life path has guided me. Allow me to participate in your transformation from a fear-based life to one grounded in LOVE. You are LOVE! Tap into your inner wisdom and discover that you are your own expert. I remain honored and blessed" - Virginia Adams

Connect with Virginia
Virginia-Adams.com
gingersreconnection@gmail.com
+1 847 445 0092

Artwork by Christina Hladnik

I am grateful for ...

CLOSING

Congrats! You made it through an entire year of consistently practicing gratitude! Give yourself a pat on the back for showing up and committing to YOU. I want you to take a moment and think back over this past year. Think about all the wonderful things that your attitude of gratitude ushered in and write them here. Give thanks for all the lessons and opportunities to grow. Have an awareness of the beauty in all the gifts that have been delivered to you.

This is only the beginning. Over the course of this year, you have undoubtedly strengthened your gratitude muscle to the point that you're using it every day, organically and without even thinking about it. Continue to make gratitude part of your daily practice and you will continue to invite amazing things in your life.

Many blessings to you on your wonderful, amazing journey. May you live in love and peace, my friend.

In love and appreciation,

Kim Richardson

www.kimrichardson.kim

Kim Richardson
Publishing

CALL TO AUTHORS

Do you have a book inside of you that is ready for the world to see? Have you ever thought about sharing your story?

Everyone has a story and I believe that by sharing our stories, we may be of service to someone else that has had a similar experience. We all learn and grow from each other. You and your lessons are a valuable asset to this world! Nothing brings me more joy than assisting others in bringing their dreams to reality and helping others to live their best life.

Everyone has their own reason for becoming a published author. Whether you are looking to create a book to support and market your business, looking to leave your mark behind in this world, or just a burning desire to help others, I would love to assist you in your journey to becoming a published author.

It is my desire to be a part of raising the vibration of the world, helping everyone to see the love within themselves and each other. Will you join me?

Perhaps you have a book already published or ready to market. I offer many services such as; book cover design, 3D book images, marketing images for email and social media, marketing videos, all to highlight your beautiful project. Perhaps you have always dreamed of having your own card deck, I'd love to help your dreams become a reality.

If you would like to get notified of up and coming publishing opportunities, sign up to get notified here; goo.gl/MzJgUJ

I look forward to working with you! Peace, love and light,

Kim

CPSIA information can be obtained
at www.ICGtesting.com
Printed in the USA
FFHW011536271218